THE NATIONAL HOME MAINTENANCE MANUAL

▲▽▲▽▲▽▲▽▲▽

A practical guide for homeowners and homeowner associations

◆ **Updated Maintenance Items**

◆ **Information on Home Construction**

◆ **Homeowner Actions That Damage Their Homes**

◆ **Maintenance Calendar Checklist**

David E. MacLellan
George E. Wolfson, AIA

The *National Home Maintenance Manual*, is published by the Building Standards Institute, a private, non-profit corporation. It is intended to be used as a consumer guide for homeowners and homeowner associations. The recommendations for use and maintenance contained herein have not been endorsed or standardized by any federal or state agency.

First Printing: April 2003
Second Printing: February 2004
Third Printing: September 2004
Fourth Printing: January 2006
Fifth Printing: September 2008
Sixth Printing: January 2015

Handy Hammer ™ is a registered trademark of
MacLellan Media, Inc.

Building Standards Institute, 1017 L Street, Suite 560, Sacramento, CA 95814-3805
Building Standards Institute, 1718 M Street NW, Suite 368, Washington, D.C. 20036-4504
www.buildingstandardsinstitute.org

Illustrations:	Eunice Ortegon, Joe Bologna, AIA
Graphic Design:	David Grandin
Editorial Assistant:	Jenny Peterson

Table of Contents

Chapter Six – Interior Components (continued)

Chapter Seven - Utility Systems

Chapter Eight - Grounds

Chapter Nine - Miscellaneous

A Message from Dave MacLellan
Author and National Home Maintenance Expert

 When George Wolfson and I wrote the first edition of this book in late 2002, our objective was to create a user-friendly text, and not a manual that would sit on the shelf and gather dust. George is an architect/builder and I am an engineer/builder, so it would be easy for us to get carried away on a technical type of publication. We were happy that the result was an entry level book that dealt with home maintenance in a very fundamental, but practical manner. Since 2002, we've sold 60,000 copies. Along the way, we've gotten some great feedback from our readers, and we have made revisions and updates nearly every two years.

For the past 40 years, I've either been building new houses or remodeling old ones, and maintaining my houses in the process. As I travel through America's residential communities, I am delighted to see older homes that have been well maintained, and I am disappointed to see ones that have fallen into disrepair. What is it about home maintenance that some owners embrace while others treat it like the plague?

First off, home maintenance is a commitment to lifestyle and value. A warm, leak-free house with a solid foundation will provide a more comfortable lifestyle than a home with all those problems. Plus, the added bonus is that the home will likely sell quicker and for a higher price if it has been properly maintained.

Second, our other objective in writing *The National Home Maintenance Manual* was to keep home maintenance SIMPLE. Describe the fundamental maintenance tasks, and then put them into chart form at the back of the book. This handy chart tells you what needs to be done, how often it should be done, and the degree of difficulty of the task. So whether you are at ease doing the work, or whether you hire a professional to do it, the information is here to achieve the desired end result. Further, beginning with this edition, our publisher is making available a free downloadable chart of year-by-year maintenance tasks for the first 10 years of a home's life! Go to www.HouseFixIt.com for your free download. And while you're there, check out our other publications on construction standards and home performance tolerances.

Remember, as with money or health, **"an ounce of maintenance is worth a pound of repair."**

Enjoy this book,

David E. MacLellan

Dave MacLellan

How To Use This Manual

The maintenance guidelines and recommendations found within this Manual, both for individual owners and homeowners' associations, are not intended to be all-inclusive. More comprehensive and detailed material on the subject of maintenance and repair can be found in the Reference Section on page 128. The recommended maintenance items in each section are minimum tasks, in the opinion of the authors, to preserve and enhance the value of your home. Terms that you may not be familiar with are printed in *blue*. When you see a word printed in *blue*, it means that the word is defined in the Glossary at the back of

this Manual. It is important to note that skill levels for performing maintenance and repair vary widely among homeowners. A homeowner should not attempt to perform any maintenance or repair task that he or she has not previously performed. For example, if a homeowner has never cleaned leaves out of the gutter or has never operated an extension ladder reaching to two stories on a house, the homeowner should have this task done by a qualified maintenance professional. If any doubt exists, the homeowner should hire an experienced maintenance

INTRODUCING
HANDY HAMMER
AND YOUR
NEW HOME

professional or they should enroll in a maintenance and repair course.

The authors have diligently attempted to research and identify conditions commonly encountered in residential maintenance. In addition to their own experience, the authors consulted with numerous homebuilding industry organizations and technical support groups. Persons interested in providing additional content are invited to express their comments to the authors at their web address: www.HouseFixIt.com for possible inclusion in future editions of this Manual. Neither the builder, the authors, nor the publishers assume any liability for claims of injury, death, or property damage resulting from the use of this Manual.

Get To Know Your Home

Getting to know your home, and becoming familiar with the surrounding grounds, is a significant first step in home ownership. This may not be your first home or you may be a subsequent purchaser of a home that was built by an experienced and professional builder. In any event, it is important that you read this Manual and follow the maintenance recommendations.

If you are a buyer of a home built by an experienced and professional builder, you will have or have had an opportunity to walk through your home with a company representative prior to closing. This process known as a "walkthrough" in the homebuilding industry, is essential. The builder's representative is trained to acquaint you with the features of your home, and to answer any questions you may have. It is a good idea to develop a list of your questions, and those of your family

THE WALKTHROUGH IS ONE OF THE MOST IMPORTANT STEPS IN TAKING DELIVERY OF THE HOUSE.

members, and set aside an adequate amount of time to learn about your home. You will learn about the operation of the heating and cooling systems, security system (if installed), appliances, fireplaces (if installed) and the builder's limited warranty, to name a few. If you are buying the home with one or more other persons, it is important that all owners be present for the walkthrough. The questions and concerns that another owner, if more than one, or those questions that a spouse may have are likely to be different from yours.

The Authors

David E. MacLellan

David MacLellan has been a "hands-on" homebuilder since 1969. He has constructed nearly all types of housing, including apartments, condominiums, townhouses, mobile home parks, planned unit developments, semi-custom homes, and custom homes. Mr. MacLellan is an engineering graduate from Penn State University with both bachelor's and master's degrees. He is licensed in California and Oregon as a general and specialty building contractor. As a frequent speaker on the subject of construction problems and their remedies, Mr. MacLellan has lectured to numerous professional groups, including the Pacific Coast Builders Conference, the North Carolina Homebuilders Association and the Homebuilders Association of Bucks County, Pennsylvania. He has founded 17 homeowner associations, and he served for nine years as President of the homeowner's association in the community where he lives. Mr. MacLellan has provided testimony in more than 300 lawsuits or disputes involving construction problems. He has been appointed as a Superior Court Referee concerning matters of land use and construction defects. His consulting firm, Pacific InterWest Building Consultants, Inc., which performs reviews of architectural plans and provides private inspection services during construction, operates in California, Oregon and Washington. Recently, Mr. MacLellan was inducted into the California Homebuilding Foundation Hall of Fame.

George E. Wolfson, AIA

George Wolfson is a licensed architect, general building contractor, and real estate broker whose professional career spans more than three decades. Mr. Wolfson holds both bachelor's and master's degrees in architecture from the University of Houston and Columbia University respectively. His professional interest area within The American Institute of Architects includes Codes and Practices. As a principal in the consulting firm, Building Performance Network, Mr. Wolfson has engaged in over 300 operations, including field investigations, destructive testing, providing remedial architectural drawings and mediating disputes between owners and builders. He has co-authored three industry publications with David MacLellan: *The California Building Performance Guidelines for Residential Construction, The National Home Maintenance Manual,* and *The Handbook of Specifications and Scopes of Work for Trade Contractors*.

If Your Home is Located in a Conventional Subdivision

A conventional subdivision is the traditional method of building and conveying homes and lots that traces its roots in America back to the late 1800s. A conventional subdivision is different from a common interest subdivision (as discussed on page 10) in that the individual owners within the subdivision own only their interest in the property and do not share an ownership interest with other owners within the subdivision. Generally speaking, the streets, utilities, drainage systems, and sidewalks become the property of the city or county, or utility company as applicable.

The maintenance responsibilities of a homeowner in a conventional subdivision begin at the front property line, normally from the back of the city sidewalk and run to the property lines along the side yards and back yard. Sometimes, the city requires that the owners maintain the sidewalk in front of their house, even though they do not own it. There is no homeowners association, and it is up to the individual homeowner to maintain his or her own property.

In recent years, a "hybrid" type of subdivision has become a popular tool in land planning. It is called the "diminimus planned unit development" or DPUD. Like the conventional subdivision, the homeowner living in a DPUD receives a deed to his or her lot and has individual maintenance responsibility for the house. On the other hand, like a common interest subdivision, there is a homeowners association to manage and maintain a smaller number of subdivision components that may include streets, recreation centers, landscaped areas, and security gates.

If Your Home is Located in a Common Interest Subdivision

Common interest subdivisions are often master planned communities with common areas consisting of townhouses or condominiums (flats) or a combination of both designs. The method by which title to the homeowner is conveyed can be complex and lengthy and is beyond the scope of this Manual. However, as a general rule, the homeowner receives individual title to some portion of the building and a fractional ownership interest in the rest of the project, including the landscaped areas, streets, swimming pool, and recreation facilities. The responsibility for maintenance of the common areas, including the exterior maintenance of the buildings, falls to a homeowners association (HOA) whose board members are elected by the individual owners within the community. The responsibility for maintenance inside the townhouse or condominium generally falls to the individual owner. This is often called an "airspace" responsibility or a "paint-to-paint" responsibility.

If the buildings within the community contain decks, balconies and patios, it is highly likely that these architectural features are designated as restricted common areas. External storage facilities may also receive a similar designation. Restricted common area means that this particular area, while remaining under the control of the HOA, is to be used exclusively by the occupants of the condominium or townhouse.

The responsibilities for maintenance of individual areas, common areas, and restricted common areas, are spelled out in a document called the Declaration of Covenants, Conditions, and Restrictions (CC&Rs). The CC&Rs are recorded on your title to the property, and every homeowner receives a copy of the CC&Rs at the time of purchase. While the CC&Rs is a legal document, it is important that each homeowner become familiar with their rights and responsibilities as a member of a community association.

Who's Responsible?

Many persons who purchase a home within a townhouse or condominium community mistakenly believe that "someone else" is going to take care of all the cleaning, maintenance, and repairs for the entire project. However, it should be noted that the "someone else" responsible for nearly all of these items is a board of directors comprised of fellow homeowners. Like a small form of government, the board of the homeowners association (HOA) makes important decisions regarding monthly homeowner assessments, budgets, rules of conduct and the employment of maintenance and management companies. These decisions have a direct effect upon the quality of life and preservation of values within the community.

For maintenance responsibilities of individual owners inside their own home, the following basic maintenance guidelines are recommended:

☑ **Manufactured Products:** Follow the maintenance recommendations included in this Manual. You may also have been given maintenance and care instructions on manufactured products within your house for such items as fireplaces, water heaters, kitchen appliances, carpet, and hardwood flooring, to name a few. Take the time to learn and apply these instructions.

☑ **Plumbing Fixtures:** Keep plumbing fixture drains clean and free flowing. Use drain cleansers on a 30-day to 6 month interval. Do not put drain cleaners into a garbage disposer as the cutting blades may become corroded.

☑ **Ventilation:** Use the vent fan or open a window when bathing or showering to reduce the likelihood of mold and mildew. Wipe shower stalls and tub enclosures after use to remove excess moisture. Let the fan run for 15 minutes after bathing or showering or leave a window open (if available) to allow the room to dry. If water has spilled over the outside of the tub, wipe it up immediately. The seam between the tub base or shower pan and floor can be vulnerable to leaking and requires periodic caulking.

☑ **Balconies and Decks:** Avoid placing potted plants directly on the surface of a deck or balcony. Place plastic or decay resistant blocks (such as redwood) to keep the pot off the surface of the deck. This will allow air to circulate and allow the surface of the deck to dry completely. Use a saucer under the pot and avoid overwatering. Move pots and furniture often so that they do not remain in one location permanently. Avoid placing potted plants on the top of the deck railing. The deck railing was not made for this use and the possibility of pots falling over creates a hazard. Because decks, balconies and patios are normally restricted spaces and enclosed by fences or railings, it is important for each homeowner to monitor the condition of these surfaces. Conditions such as wobbling railings, nails pulling loose, cracks in surfaces, and rotting wood should be reported to the management company representative or a member of the board of directors.

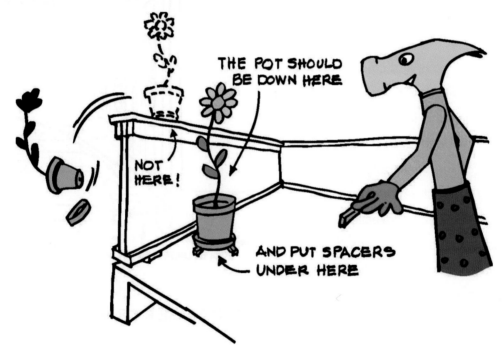

☑ **Common Area Observations:** Observe unusual and potentially damaging conditions in the common area and report them to the management company representative or to a member of the board of directors. Such conditions might include broken sprinkler heads flooding water in unintended areas; irrigation systems spraying during periods of heavy rain; trash enclosure doors broken or in bad repair; street drains and yard drains not draining freely; and pigeons and other wildfowl taking up residency.

Ten Most Common Mistakes Made by Homeowners

1. **Alteration of Finished Grades.** Alteration by the homeowner or homeowner's agent of finished grades established by the builder at the time of delivery of the house is a common problem. The grades around the house are designed to allow rain water and irrigation water to flow away from the foundation. Alteration of the grades by a homeowner or a contractor hired by a homeowner (such as a swimming pool or patio contractor) can result in house foundation movement. Unlike a condominium or planned unit development where the builder customarily installs the walkways, patios, landscaping and drainage systems, a single family residence is often

delivered to the homeowner without any of these items except a driveway. At a minimum, building regulations typically require that the house be delivered to the homeowner with the surrounding bare lot sloped away from the house at a 2% *slope*. Often, cities and counties require slopes greater than 2%. A slight V-shaped impression is cut in the lot, called a *swale*. Rainwater is intended to flow away from the house, to the swale, and then eventually to the street or some other approved storm water collection system. Unfortunately, the homeowner or an aftermarket contractor will often pour the sidewalks and patios directly on top of the finished grade, thus altering the water flow by trapping it between the walkway and the

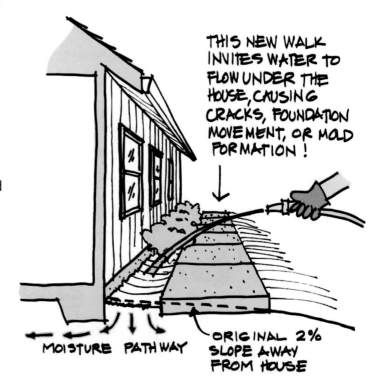

THIS NEW WALK INVITES WATER TO FLOW UNDER THE HOUSE, CAUSING CRACKS, FOUNDATION MOVEMENT, OR MOLD FORMATION !

MOISTURE PATHWAY

ORIGINAL 2% SLOPE AWAY FROM HOUSE

DO NOT ALTER ORIGINAL SITE DRAINAGE!

house. Swimming pool contractors have been known to set their decks and coping too high, causing water to flow back toward the house. Often, the net effect of altering the storm water flow around the house is storm water seepage under the foundation. Many soils that are high in clay content will not permit water to readily pass through. This means that soils remain wet and can swell (expand) to up to 30% of their dry volume. The swelling soil can actually lift the house foundation upward and cause extensive interior and exterior damage.

2. **Concrete Patio Poured Too High.** In addition to being poured with a 2% slope, a concrete patio or deck should be poured at least 2 inches below door thresholds or the stucco weep screed (a weep screed is the metal band at the bottom of the stucco just above the ground). The weep screed allows water that may be behind the stucco to "weep" out and run down the foundation. Pouring the concrete patio or deck too high can result in rainwater being drawn back into the stucco or behind the siding. As a result, decay of the structure may occur. This condition also provides an excellent route for termites to enter the building. Since the finished grade should be maintained 6 inches below the house slab, any installed concrete work should not trap water against the foundation. In addition, planters should not be allowed to fill above the required grade.

3. **Deck Trellis, Sunscreen, or Lanai Structure Improperly Attached.** This description includes other structures that are connected to the house. There are several ways to properly create a watertight connection between the deck trellis or the lanai structure and the house. Unfortunately, these "add on structures" are often just nailed or bolted directly to the outside wall of the house. Inevitably, rainwater finds its way into the penetrations and the *dryrot* process begins. It is critical that the ledger (the board that is placed up against the side of the house) be either flashed with a metal flashing or caulked in an industry approved manner. If bolts are used to attach the ledger board to the house, the bolt holes should be filled with caulk. **Note: Nearly all local governments require a building permit to construct a trellis or lanai that is attached to the house.** A trellis or lanai is considered a structure that could fall down and cause injury; hence a building permit is usually required. Although requirements vary, construction of a deck or patio typically does not require a building permit unless it is 30 inches or more off the ground. Some add-on structures, depending upon their complexity, may require the certification of a design professional such as an architect or structural engineer.

4. **Irrigation Sprinkler Heads Spray Against the House.** Irrigation sprinkler heads that spray against the wood siding, masonry, or stucco walls of a house can lead to rotted walls and leaching of the color from the stucco. Exterior walls are not constructed to withstand the rigors of constant exposure to landscape irrigation. Irrigation water that ponds at the base of a foundation can lead to upward movement of the foundation. It is important that all irrigation spray be directed away from the house rather than towards the house. Spray heads should be checked regularly during the irrigation season to make sure that they have not become twisted and point toward the house. It is also important to recognize that as landscaping grows, spray heads should be raised, relocated, or in some cases eliminated, to keep moisture away from the

side of the house. Particularly vulnerable to irrigation spray are posts from overhead decks that have shrubbery growing closely around them.

5. **Bathroom and Laundry Vent Fans Disconnected or Unused.** Bathrooms and laundries are areas of high humidity. Bathroom and laundry fans should never be disconnected (even though the noise may bother the occupant), and the fan should always be turned on during use. Failure to use the vent fans can result in water vapor getting into the drywall, the electrical outlets and even the framing members. Over time, mold, mildew and fungi may grow in these areas. Water vapor that condenses on walls and windows can eventually find its way into the structure of the house and weaken the structure through *dryrot*. Rooms where humidifiers are used should also be well ventilated.

6. **Walking on the Roof.** A homeowner should <u>never</u> walk on his or her roof. Not only can walking on the roof be a slip and fall hazard, but untrained persons are likely to break the roof covering and cause roof leaks. Most houses built today have one of three types of roof covers: concrete or clay tile, wood shakes or shingles, or composition shingles. A few houses today are constructed with "flat" roofs, sometimes known as built up roofs. Cleaning of gutters should be done from a ladder and not by standing on the roof. If an object is thrown on the roof, such as a child's toy, it should be retrieved using a ladder and a telescoping pole rather than walking on the roof. Most residential warranties exclude damage resulting from unauthorized persons walking on roofs.

7. **Upper Cabinets Overloaded.** While lower cabinets rest on the floor, upper cabinets are hung from a wall by screws or nails. By stacking heavy dishes and glassware in upper cabinets, a homeowner can load the cabinet beyond its capacity. This can result in sagging shelves or worse yet, detachment of the cabinet from the wall. Heavy china and cookware should always be placed in the lower cabinets. In a related item, cabinet drawers are often overloaded and then pulled out too far. This action results in the plastic guide being snapped off at the back of the cabinet drawer.

8. **Floor System Overloaded.** Builders have a choice of many wooden floor systems to install in their homes. Regardless of system chosen, all systems must meet the minimum requirements for floor deflection (up and down movement) that are set forth in the building code. Many homeowners are surprised to learn the building code permits more deflection than that which

they may be comfortable. Household items such as waterbeds, aquariums, pool tables, and weight lifting equipment can cause significant floor deflection, even though the house was built in accordance with the code. Many houses have a concrete slab first floor and a wooden second floor. If possible, it is best to keep heavy items on the first floor, particularly if the first floor is a concrete slab.

9. **Storage of Household Goods on the Garage and Attic Trusses.** The garage and attic *trusses* are designed to support the weight of the roof and ceiling and not the weight of anything else. Unfortunately, many homeowners view the space in the attic and above the garage ceiling as additional space for storage. Storing household goods in these areas can result in sagging of the roof or possible collapse of the roof. If a homeowner wishes to use this space for storage, he or she should consult with a structural engineer to determine if additional reinforcement is necessary.

DO NOT USE ATTIC FOR STORAGE
-IT WASN'T DESIGNED FOR THAT USE!

10. **Tinting of Dual Pane Windows.** Most homes are constructed with dual pane windows (also known as double-glazed or insulating windows). The two panes of glass are separated by a spacer up to 5/8-inch thickness. The air space between the dual panes is "dead air". This area is so tightly sealed that air can neither enter nor leave the space. By placing a tinting film on the <u>inside</u> of the window, the sun's rays are reflected back into the dead air space. The temperature in this space can become so hot that it may cause the "rubber-like" seal to rupture, and the insulating value of the window is lost. Windows with broken or ruptured seals are easy to identify: they have moisture between the panes of glass. Homeowners should never tint a dual pane window on the inside unless specifically approved by the window manufacturer.

Additional Problems to be Avoided by Homeowners

☒ **Hanging a Ceiling Fan From a Light Fixture Box.**
Light fixture boxes in the ceiling are not designed to carry the weight of a ceiling fan. Ceiling fans have a special mounting box that requires a different mounting system than a typical light fixture box. If a ceiling fan is hung from a light fixture box, the vibration and the weight of the fan may cause the box to rip out of the ceiling. Ceiling fans also have special electrical connection requirements that differ from ordinary light fixtures.

☒ **Placing Plastic Deflectors Over Furnace Vents.**
Furnace vents, known as warm air supply grills, are often placed in front of a window or slider door (either in the floor or ceiling). They are designed to sweep the air from these areas and mix it with the air in the center of the room. By placing plastic deflectors over the grills, the homeowner creates a space of stagnant air with high humidity during the rainy season. Moisture condenses on the windows and over time, can rot the windowsills and structural members inside the wall. Mold and mildew are likely to grow in these areas. Plastic deflectors should never be used on warm air supply grills.

☒ **Cracking Fireplace Linings.**
Generally, fireplace linings are two types: a cast panel of simulated brick or real brick with mortar between each brick. All fireplaces require a series of low heat fires to "cure" the fireplace lining. By initially building a very hot fire (such as burning sawdust, wax logs, newspapers, or gift wrappings), intense heat can be generated and cause the fireplace lining to crack. Never burn paper or other composite products in the fireplace. Be certain to follow the manufacturer's instructions at all times.

☒ **Placing Rugs or Non-breathable Coverings Over Wood and Synthetic Decks.**
Decks need to breathe, even decks with synthetic coatings. By placing non-breathable coverings (such as indoor/outdoor carpeting) over wood and synthetic decks, moisture will be trapped between the bottom of the covering and the top of the deck. This can result in rot and premature failure of the deck.

☒ **Security Alarm Installation / Penetration of Windows and Walls.**
If an aftermarket alarm is installed by the homeowner or by a contractor who has not been hired by the builder, great care should be taken to seal all penetrations through windows and walls to avoid future dryrot. Never drill into the bottom track of a window or door to install an alarm contact.

☒ **Spraying A Hose On Exterior Doors.**
Homeowners often make the mistake of trying to clean their exterior doors by spraying a hose on them. Exterior doors are not designed to repel water from hose washing. All too often, the homeowner discovers that the hardwood or tile entry has warped or buckled as a result of water going under the threshold. Doors can be cleaned with a dusting brush and, if necessary, a damp turkish towel.

☒ **Nailing Fences to House Walls.**
Nailing any part of a fence to a house wall invites two problems: trapping rainwater between the fence post and the house wall, and the invasion of termites through the fence into the house structure. The terminating fence post should be placed in the ground beside the foundation and should not be attached to or come in contact with the house.

Winterizing Your Home

General Subject Information:

Houses that are built in climate zones that experience snow and below-freezing temperatures are constructed somewhat differently to accommodate adverse weather conditions. Additional components, such as reinforced roof structures to handle a snow load, extra insulation packages, special plumbing design and components, and eave strip heaters, are some examples of cold climate specialty building.

Home maintenance in cold climate zones is particularly important to prevent damage that can occur during extreme weather conditions. The primary damage to houses in sub-freezing regions is water damage from ruptured and unprotected pipes. Another source of water damage comes from melting snow that has been piled against doors and foundation walls. A third cause of damage stems from a structural failure of a roof system that is unable to support the weight of heavy wet snow.

The following guidelines assist a homeowner to perform maintenance and take preventative measures to prevent damage to the house during winter months and spring thaws:

- ☑ **Gutter Cleanout.** If the house is equipped with gutters, they should be cleaned thoroughly when the fall leaf drop is complete. Blocked gutters that do not drain freely are likely to back up and can pass water into the eave of the roof.

- ☑ **Garden Hoses.** Remove all garden hoses from the exterior hose faucet (called a hose bib) even though the house may be equipped with a special freeze resistant hose bib. These special faucets will fail (burst) if they cannot drain freely from the shut off point inside the house to the exterior. A hose attached to the house bib prevents drainage from occurring.

- ☑ **Foundation Vents.** If the house has a raised floor foundation (not a slab), it will have foundation vents around the perimeter. In sub-zero weather, these vents should be closed and foam blocks should be placed into the vent opening to provide additional insulation and blockage of cold winds. Cold air blowing into the crawl space can freeze the pipes in that area.

- ☑ **Irrigation System.** A landscape irrigation system should be properly prepared for winter. This is typically done by a specialist who will open all the valves, and using compressed air, blow any trapped water out of the piping. An irrigation system that is not prepared in this manner is likely to suffer broken pipes and sprinkler heads, which are unfortunately discovered during spring start-up.

☑ **Drain-Downs.** A drain-down is a valve that is located on the lowest part of the water supply system. When the water to the house is shut off at the street, a drain-down valve can be opened, and it will drain out the water that is in the house piping system. In the event of a total loss of heat (see below), a drain-down is a valuable addition to any plumbing system to prevent thousands of dollars of water damage. If the house does not have a drain-down, a homeowner should contact a plumber to have one installed.

☑ **Lowered Heat.** Unless the house is going to be closed for winter where the water would be shut off, the plumbing system drained down, and all sink traps and toilets filled with antifreeze, the house can perform well under a lowered thermostat setting. For extended periods when the house is unoccupied, setting the thermostat at 55 degrees is sufficient in most cases to prevent pipes from freezing and bursting.

☑ **Plumbing On Exterior Walls.** If plumbing is run in exterior walls to a fixture such as a kitchen sink, the sink cabinet doors should be left open while the homeowner is not in residence. By keeping the cabinet doors open, heated air can circulate into the cabinet space and keep the pipes from freezing.

☑ **Snow Drifts.** Snow that is allowed to drift up against exterior doors, windows, and garage doors will eventually melt. Doors in particular are especially susceptible to snow melt leaking through the weather stripping and under the threshold. Weep holes on windows can also back up. These house components were not designed to repel water under such conditions. It is important that the homeowner keep snow away from these openings.

☑ **Total Loss Of Heat.** A total loss of heat typically occurs from a power failure. An electric power failure will cause a gas furnace to stop operating because both the thermostat and the gas regulator valves are electrically controlled. Another reason for a total loss of heat is the failure of the heat source itself within the house, such as the furnace or a heat pump. The former condition puts the homeowner at the mercy of the utility company, while the latter condition can be handled by calling a heating contractor. A homeowner is wise to have another heat source such as a fireplace or environmentally compliant wood or pellet stove. Heat sources that do not vent to the outdoors, such as kerosene heaters, catalytic heaters or any appliance that burns fossil fuels and is not vented to the outside of the house, are not recommended. They often produce poisonous gases as part of their operation. If a loss of heat is lengthy enough to cause the inside temperature of the house to reach 40 degrees Fahrenheit, the water supply to the house should be shut off at the water meter and the plumbing system should be drained down.

Aftermarket Contractors

At the time a subdivision of homes nears completion and homeowners are beginning to occupy their homes, business opportunities arise for aftermarket contractors. Typically, these contractors have no relationship with the original builder or their subcontractors. Aftermarket contractors often provide goods and services such as swimming pools, security systems, landscaping, deck, patio and masonry work. Aftermarket contractors can perform valuable services that may add to the beauty and enjoyment of the house. Since these contractors were generally not involved in the original design and construction of the house, it is important that you pay special attention to the work they perform. If the aftermarket work is not carefully integrated into the original construction, problems may arise that could potentially lead to unsatisfactory performance of your house.

Unfortunately, many aftermarket contractors are not licensed. Most states require any person or company performing residential improvement work to possess a valid and current contractor's license. For the most part, ordinary household repair work is exempted from the license requirement. However, nearly all aftermarket work on a house requires a license. In many cases, it also requires a building permit.

WARNING!

Often times an unlicensed contractor's pitch to a homeowner is:

☒ A license is not needed for the work that we do;
☒ We can do it cheaper because we're not licensed;
☒ No building permit is needed for this work.

The lure of a cheap price often results in shoddy and incomplete workmanship. An unlicensed contractor typically carries no insurance and does not pay payroll taxes. Further, it is a misdemeanor in many states for any person (such as a homeowner) to knowingly enter into a contract, either oral or written, with an unlicensed contractor. This is called aiding and abetting an unlicensed contractor. A homeowner should always deal with a licensed contractor. Most states have a governing department or board that licenses and regulates contractors. Before signing any contract it is wise to verify with your state agency that:

- The contractor holds a current license or is not required to do so;
- There is no disciplinary action taken against the contractor;

- The contractor is properly licensed for the specialty work he proposes to perform (i.e., electrical wiring, plumbing, swimming pools).

You should also require the contractor to provide a current certificate of general liability and workers compensation insurance. The insurance certificates should become part of, and be maintained with your <u>written</u> contract.

Chapter One

FOUNDATIONS

includes:

Slab on Grade

Grade Beam and Pier

Sulfates

Basements

oundations

General Subject Information: The majority of houses are built on slab foundations. These foundations consist of reinforced concrete that is poured on a prepared grade. Reinforcing can consist of steel rods called *rebar* or welded wire mesh, or the reinforcing can be cables that are stretched tight after pouring the concrete. This is known as a post tensioned slab. Another popular type of foundation is known as the grade beam and pier system. This system consists of *piers* drilled into the ground and filled with reinforcing steel and concrete. The piers are connected to low concrete perimeter and interior walls. Some homes have basements that consist of a room or rooms below the ground level. Footing and stem wall foundations with a crawl space are also a common practice.

Slab on Grade

Comments: Concrete cracks for many reasons. The worst cracks are caused by expansive (clay like) soils that shrink or expand based upon water content in the soil. Cracking is an inherent characteristic of a cement product. Soil expansion related cracks usually appear as vertical displacement rather than horizontal cracks that stay in the same plane. For slab-on-grade floors, a small amount of moisture under the slab is beneficial because it keeps the soil from drying out and shrinking.

Recommended Use and Maintenance:
- ✓ The finished grade along the foundation must *slope* a minimum of ¼ inch per 1-foot away from the foundation to allow for proper drainage. Do not alter the finished grade.
- ✓ It is recommended that you install *drip irrigation* along the foundation for better water control. This will eliminate any over-spray onto the house or concrete foundation.
- ✓ Periodic inspections of the irrigation system, materials, and slopes are necessary for proper and adequate maintenance.
- ✓ If rain is forecast, you should put the irrigation controller on "RAIN" setting.
- ✓ Every fall, test your downspout drains with a garden hose to make sure that they are free-flowing.

Grade Beam and Pier

Recommended Use and Maintenance:
- ✓ Keep all wood or paper products from beneath the house and away from the foundation. Do not store wood or paper products in the crawl space. Wood material attracts termites and encourages infestation within the structure of the house.
- ✓ Avoid attaching anything wooden to the house (such as a fence post) if it makes contact with the earth.
- ✓ If you consider the *efflorescence* on the concrete surface to be unsightly, it can be removed with a brush and water. For more stubborn areas, brush area with a mixture of one cup of white vinegar to a bucket of water.

Sulfates

General Subject Information: The effect of sulfates in the soil on concrete has been researched and debated for more than 70 years and is still not totally understood. Sulfate exposure can be a result of an "external" or "internal" source. External sources are the naturally occurring sulfates in the environment. Another external source are those sulfates that are a product of industrial processes or various human activities, i.e. fertilizers used in landscaping. A third external source is excessive ground water combined with minerals in the surrounding soils that are incompatible with the concrete mix. Internal sources of sulfates may include the sulfates introduced in the concrete; i.e. "dirty aggregate" (rock) from which concrete is made. Despite multiple sources, the potential for sulfate causing structural problems is extremely small.

Recommended Use and Maintenance:

- ✓ Do not use fertilizers that are high in sulfates in or around foundations.
- ✓ Watering around concrete, specifically foundations, should be kept to a minimum. Do not flood areas adjacent to foundations. Excessive irrigation will cause problems.
- ✓ Keeping adequate drainage away from the building foundation is an important maintenance item.

ONLY USE SULFATE-FREE FERTILIZER NEAR THE HOUSE

Basements

General Subject Information: A basement is the portion of the house that extends below the surrounding grade. Basements can be partial (usually found in houses built on hillsides) or full (completely under the first floor). Full basements often built in Midwestern and Eastern homes are uncommon in homes built in the western United States. Crawl spaces do not qualify as basements. Additionally, basements are usually constructed for two distinct uses: utility or habitability. Examples of utility are storage, workshop, laundry, and location of mechanical equipment. Examples of habitability are au pair setup, bonus room, bedroom, home theater, and arts and crafts room.

Typically, basements consist of poured concrete walls or concrete block walls and a concrete slab floor. Because the basement is below grade, care must be taken during construction (and thereafter by the homeowner) to limit moisture intrusion. A basement that is built and marketed as habitable space (or future habitable space) is likely to have finished wall and floor coverings placed over their concrete surfaces. In other words, the slab of a habitable basement floor is considered the same as a slab-on-grade floor; habitable basement walls are considered the same as upstairs walls. Basements often have sump pumps to collect and pump out water that seeps in from the higher surrounding ground.

Comments: Because basements are built below grade, they will be damp in winter months. Basements built for utility purposes do not have the same requirements for heating, cooling and ventilation as habitable basements. Condensation on basement walls should not be confused with an actual leak from the outside.

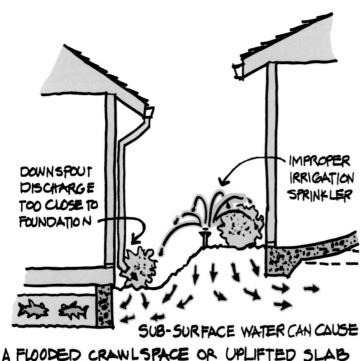

DOWNSPOUT DISCHARGE TOO CLOSE TO FOUNDATION

IMPROPER IRRIGATION SPRINKLER

SUB-SURFACE WATER CAN CAUSE A FLOODED CRAWLSPACE OR UPLIFTED SLAB

DO NOT ALTER THE DRAINAGE!

Recommended Use and Maintenance:

✓ Avoid making any changes to the surrounding grades that would cause rain or irrigation water to flow down the outside of the basement walls. This includes over-watering, constructing planter beds without independent drainage, building "dams" between foundations and raised walkways and failure to keep *swales* and yard drains cleaned out.

✓ If basement dampness is an issue, installation of a dehumidifier may help.

✓ In no event should the moisture barrier on the outside of the basement wall be damaged when planting or irrigation is installed.

✓ If your basement has a sump pump, during the drier months pour water into the sump and verify that the float switches turn the pump on and that the discharge line remains clean and free flowing.

Chapter Two

FLOORS & CEILINGS

includes:

Floor Squeaks

Exterior Wood Beams / Posts

25

Floors and Ceilings

Floor Squeaks

General Subject Information: Floors and ceilings begin their formation during the "rough" carpentry stage of house construction. Rough carpentry generally deals with the structural portion of a building that supports the floors, ceilings, walls and roofs. Finish floor coverings are discussed in Chapter Six, Interior Components. Usually the rough carpentry is covered up by an assortment of interior and exterior finishes, including, but not limited to: drywall, plaster, paneling, stucco, siding, brick veneer and floor coverings (i.e. carpet, vinyl or hardwood). Lumber used for decks that is exposed to the weather will need scheduled maintenance in order to eliminate premature aging and deterioration.

Recommended Use and Maintenance:

✓ Floor squeaks are likely to occur with seasonal weather changes, and they usually become a maintenance item. Squeaky floors can be maintained in three ways:
1) If the first floor has a crawl space beneath it, a wood shim can be placed between the underside of the subfloor and the nearest structural member (called a joist);
2) If the squeak is on the upper floors, the carpet can be taken back and a wood screw is put through the floor joist at the location of the squeak; and
3) To be performed by a professional: A large finish nail can be driven through the carpet, into the subfloor and into the joist below. Care should be taken when nailing or screwing through a subfloor so that no electrical, plumbing, or air conditioning components are encountered.

Do not store excessively heavy objects on a wood subfloor. Heavy objects such as water beds and slate bedded pool tables should be placed over a load bearing wall if possible. Placement in the middle of a room (unless the subfloor is concrete) can lead to permanent floor sagging.

Exterior Wood Beams and Posts

Comments: It should be noted that exposed wood posts and beams are natural materials and are subject to splitting. This is considered normal. All lumber is grade stamped as to its level of quality. If the lumber is free from heart material, it will most likely resist splitting. The typical material used for post and beams meets the structural requirements, but not necessarily meets concerns with appearance. When beams or posts twist in a minor but normal manner, they generally do not create any potential structural problems. However, if a beam ties into a vertical wall and twisting occurs, it may create an opportunity for water intrusion. It should also be noted that exposed lumber is subject to moisture and will expand and contract in accordance with air moisture levels. Splitting is usually not considered a structural concern, but more of an appearance issue.

Recommended Use and Maintenance:

✓ All exterior lumber should be inspected annually for any caulking separation or peeling of paint and should be immediately repaired in order to prevent future problems. You can fill small splits with any number of commercially available wood fillers.
✓ If significant **dryrot** is observed, a structural specialist should be consulted to see if the beam or post needs replacing.

Chapter Three

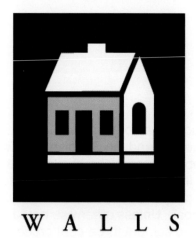

W A L L S

includes:

Stucco

Weep Screed and Wood Trim

Exterior Insulation and Finish System (EIFS)

Siding:
Composite Wood
Panel
Vinyl
Cement Board

Walls

Stucco Walls

General Subject Information: Stucco is a coating material that is applied to the exterior of the house. Its origin is traced to both Europe and the Spanish southwest, where a crude mixture of adobe clay, sand and water was applied over adobe bricks. By the 1920s, stucco consisted of portland cement, sand, and water. It was applied by hand troweling and later by hose nozzles. Wood or metal lath held the stucco to the vertical walls. It was applied in three coats known as scratch, brown, and finish or color coat. Unless otherwise noted in this Manual, the term "stucco" refers to the above-described portland cement three-coat process and is normally 7/8-inch thick.

A second finish system, known as the one-coat system, has gained popularity in recent years. This method of exterior finish consists of a foam board applied to the studs or sheathing of the house frame. Next, metal wire lath is stapled to the foam boards, and a fiber cement product is applied with trowels or by spraying. Lastly, a finish coat consisting of colored stucco or acrylic paint is applied. The thickness of the one-coat is about 3/8-inch plus the thickness of the foam board.

A third system, known as Exterior Insulation and Finish Systems (EIFS) was introduced to the United States in the late 1970s. EIFS are a type of cladding for exterior building walls that provide a surface (resembling stucco) in an integrated composite system. EIFS typically consist of a foam board adhesively and/or mechanically attached over a continuous rigid undersurface board-like material, continuous fiberglass mesh embedded in a polymer-based basecoat, and a finish or color coat made of a 100% acrylic paint-like material, provides color and texture.

Comments: Why does stucco crack? When houses are built, the wood framing materials contain up to 19% moisture. As the lumber dries, the wood shrinks and causes stress to the stucco system. As the house ages, components expand and contract at different rates, placing stress on the weaker materials. Expansion and contraction is an inherent characteristic of a wood structure. (*Have you ever noticed that sometimes a wood door sticks, yet other times it opens and closes smoothly? That is because the wood expands and contracts as a result of moisture content in the air*). When the building structure expands and contracts during the settling period, stucco is certain to crack in predictable locations. This condition should be expected and is considered normal.

Stucco can also crack during the application process if it *cures* too quickly or if it is not allowed to cure between coats. Stucco is a very hard and unforgiving material with no elasticity or elongation properties with respect to movement. Cracking is very common at the corners of door and window frames and anywhere there is a hinging effect within the rough framing of the structure. These particular areas are considered "hinge points" in the framing, and induce stress to the hard, but brittle, stucco finish. If and when cracks appear in the walls and soffits, it is not a condition to cause concern. Most cracks in stucco can be easily maintained by the homeowner.

Appearance Issues:
♦ Because stucco is a semi-porous material, it will retain water after a storm. The special paper that is behind stucco acts as a water resistant membrane to prevent moisture from entering the house. The rate of the stucco drying after a storm will not be uniform.

♦ It is also normal for stucco walls to have a wavy appearance under low or artificial lighting. Stucco is a cement mixture that is applied to walls with a trowel or spray gun. The final finish will not be perfectly flat, and structural elements such as studs or structural panel joints may "reflect" through the finish.

Recommended Use and Maintenance:

✔ Do not alter the finished grades around the perimeter of the house. Undrained, wet soil can cause foundation movement and result in stucco cracking.

✔ Expect some normal cracking in stucco.

✔ The white powdery substance (known as efflorescence) that appears on stucco walls and bare concrete slabs during the rainy season is caused by lime in the cement reacting with moist air. It is considered normal and can easily be removed with water and a brush.

Weep Screed and Wood Trim

Comments: Weep screeds are strips of metal and are used as part of stucco applications. They run parallel to and about 6 inches off the ground where the stucco terminates. Rainwater that may be trapped behind the stucco will run down the building paper and exit through the weep screed. Over time, *weep screeds* may rust. Unlike roof flashing and other exterior flashing, the weep screed is not primed and painted to allow for future protection from the elements. Weep screeds serve three purposes: (1) as a gauge for the thickness of the stucco, (2) to allow the application of the stucco to be in a straight line, and (3) to provide an avenue for moisture that is trapped behind the stucco to exit at the base of the wall. Rust marks on weep screeds usually indicate a *bleed through* of rusted lath or nails in the stucco. Some of these rust marks are inevitable.

The term "trim" refers to the wooden trim which either abuts the masonry or stucco, or is placed on the siding around windows and doors as part of the architectural features of the house. Beams and other structural members are embedded into stucco for the same reason. Much of the trim wood is "keyed" by having the stucco side beveled back or grooved to accept a tight fit between stucco and wood.

Recommended Use and Maintenance:

✔ Keep irrigation water from spraying against the stucco. Do not allow vegetation to overgrow in the screed area.

✔ **Do not fasten** any objects to the walls and soffits that are not properly *flashed, counterflashed* and sealed.

✔ Around the foundation, maintain a minimum clearance of 4 inches from finished grade to weep screed and a 2-inch minimum clearance between concrete/asphalt and the weep screed.

✔ Maintain a minimum *slope* of ¼-inch per foot away from the house (foundation) on both soil and hard surfaces.

✔ It is very important to inspect for gaps and, if required, caulk around all wood members with a 25-year rated caulk before the rainy season

AVOID THIS NIGHTMARE...
AVOID WALL LEAKS!

begins. Any old caulking should be removed completely before re-caulking the area.

✓ The wood trim should be inspected each year prior to the start of the rainy season. As wood trim dries, gaps between the wood and stucco may develop.

✓ If the trim has pulled away from the house or the caulking has deteriorated, these areas should be re-caulked. If warping or twisting is severe (more than ½-inch), the trim should be replaced. Some caulking may even be required in locations not originally installed by the builder.

EIFS (Exterior Insulation and Finish System)

General Subject Information: EIFS are exterior applied finish systems that look similar to stucco. However, initial appearance is where the similarities end. EIFS is made up of sheets of EPS (extruded polystyrene) that can be either mechanically or adhesively fastened to solid backing board material. Fiberglass mesh is embedded into a thin layer of cement-like material. A finish coat of acrylic, when combined with the fiberglass, creates a waterproofing material and is then applied as the finish coat.

Recommended Use and Maintenance:
✓ Do not nail, screw or tie into any portion of the exterior finish. Any fastening into the system must be performed by a certified EIFS installer, for that particular manufactured system.

✓ All exterior landscape irrigation must be installed and maintained in such a way as to not permit any water to spray directly onto the wall system.

✓ It should be noted that the EIFS system is susceptible to dings and gouges, so you should take extra precaution to protect the EIFS system from such damage.

Hardboard Siding

General Subject Information: There are a number of siding products on the market that are made of various wood fiber materials. It is impractical to cover them all individually. The information that follows is generally applicable to these types of products. This section concentrates primarily on siding made of wood particles or other wood based products that are mixed with a resin to bind them together. Most of these siding systems are intended to look like horizontal wood siding and are often embossed to create a wood grain appearance on the surface.

Comments: Siding materials are subject to swelling at the lower or "drip" edge of each lap when the core material is exposed to and absorbs excessive moisture. This swelling is commonly known as "brooming." In order to avoid "brooming", it is essential to prevent moisture from entering composite wood

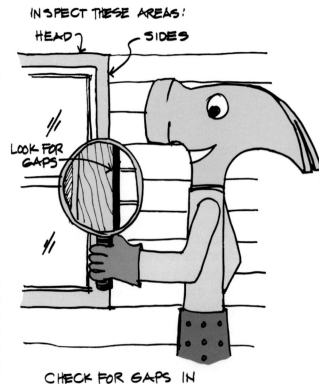

INSPECT THESE AREAS!

HEAD — — SIDES

LOOK FOR GAPS

CHECK FOR GAPS IN WINDOW TRIM CAULKING

material at the drip edge. This can only be done if the drip edge is properly coated with 100% acrylic paint. This coating should be main-tained by the homeowner as part of a scheduled maintenance program.

Recommended Use and Maintenance:

✓ It is important to observe the condition of painted siding surfaces on a periodic basis. An annual inspection is recommended. When paints begin to show signs of wear it usually occurs in limited areas. Regular maintenance and touch up painting before paint degradation worsens will significantly extend the life of the siding system. Among other things this involves painting the siding on a regular schedule (as provided in the manufacturer's recommendations), and re-caulking joints periodically.

✓ It is important to make sure that exposure to earth, paved surfaces, and water are properly controlled. Prevent irrigation heads from spraying onto siding. When landscape improvements are installed, take care to maintain the original clearances. You are also responsible for proper maintenance of systems that can adversely affect the siding.

✓ Siding nails should be inspected annually. Rusting nail heads can be sealed with a clear aerosol sealer. An exterior painting schedule should be followed to ensure proper maintenance. See "Paint and Stain" in Chapter Five.

Panel Siding

General Subject Information: Panel siding typically consists of plywood or hardboard installed in pieces ranging from 4 x 4 feet or 4 x 8 or 9 feet. Often the outer surface of the plywood sheet has been "textured" by resawing or by embossing. Also, the surface may have grooves cut into it to simulate boards or wide channels to simulate *battens*. This type of siding is often found on the sides and back of the house.

Recommended Use and Maintenance:

✓ Refer to the previous maintenance instructions in the Composite Wood Siding Section.

Vinyl Siding

General Subject Information: Vinyl siding is becoming popular as one of the alternatives to hardboard siding. Vinyl siding is a lightweight, non-wood product that is manufactured with integral color and is resistant to wood destroying insects. Also, many vinyl siding products can be painted.

Recommended Use and Maintenance:

✓ Refer to the manufacturer's care instructions and warranty on vinyl siding.

Cement Board Siding

General Subject Information: Cement board siding is another popular alternative to composite wood siding. Relatively new to the building market, cement board siding offers the advantages of being fire and moisture resistant, and is also resistant to wood destroying insects. The disadvantage to cement board siding it is prone to cracking if not properly installed.

<u>Recommended Use and Maintenance</u>:

✓ Perform an annual inspection of your siding and look for cracks and nails that have backed out. Cracks can be caulked and painted. Nails that have backed out should be pulled out and replaced with a slightly larger nail that has a hot dip galvanized coating. Be sure not to overdrive the nail because you can crack the siding. The underside of the nail head should fit snugly into the siding. If the nail head is flush with the siding surface, it has been hammered in too far.

Chapter Four

R O O F S

includes:

Flashing and Counterflashing

Structural Components

Concrete and Clay Tiles, Slate

Composition Asphalt Shingles

Wood Shake and Shingle Roofs

Composite or Synthetic Roof System

Roof Ventilation

Eaves

Built Up and other Low Slope Roofs

Roofs

General Subject Information: Many different materials are available for application to residential roofs. Reasons for choosing a particular material include geographic location of the structure, typical anticipated climatic conditions, slope or angle of incline of the roof, appearance considerations, and desired life span of the roof system. All of the different materials encompass a range of performance characteristics, including their anticipated life spans. Information regarding recommended configurations, installation methods, maintenance practices and repair procedures can usually be obtained from the material manufacturer or from a recognized industry association.

In the absence of a brochure, how do you know who the tile, shake, or shingle manufacturer was, and how the roof cover was supposed to be installed? Some manufacturers stamp their name on the back of their roofing material. If there is no identification, a sample can also be taken to a roofing supply company to obtain the information. Nearly all manufacturers publish information about the proper method for installation of their product.

Roofs can generally be separated into two broad categories: low-slope (often referred to as "flat" roofs), and steep slope (generally having more than 3 inches per foot of *slope*). Steep-slope roofs are typically fitted with water-shedding roof covering systems. These roof covering systems include asphalt shingles, clay or concrete tile, slate, wood or composite shakes, wood or composite shingles, and sheet metal panels. Low-slope roofs are typically covered with a waterproof membrane roof system, such as hot asphalt built up roofs (BUR). Low-slope roofs are then surfaced with gravel, embedded mineral granules or field-applied coatings, modified asphalt roof *membranes*, and single-ply roof membranes (which are typically smooth surfaced and have water tight, sealed seams).

Except for desert locations, most residential roofs are usually built as steep-slope, water shedding systems. At slopes less than 3 inches per foot, special consideration should be given to design and installation of water shedding roof-covering materials.

Flashing and Counterflashing

General Subject Information: Sheet metal *flashing* or *counterflashing* components provide a mechanical overlap that protects terminations or transitions of roofing materials (e.g., at plumbing vent pipes, skylight curbs, roof edges and the base of walls) from wind-driven rain or runoff water. Water is conveyed by the flashing past the transition or termination where it passes onto the roof covering downslope or off the roof.

Structural Components

Recommended Use and Maintenance:
- ✓ You should not install or fasten any products or materials on the roof. Consult with the builder prior to the installation of any "add-on" materials, including the installation of solar heating panels and TV antenna dishes.
- ✓ Limit the amount of walking on the roof. Concrete and clay tile roofs are susceptible to breakage and only licensed persons qualified to walk on roofs should perform any installation of "add-on" products.

Concrete and Clay Tiles, Slate

Comments: Roof tiles and slate are a protective and decorative cover and are generally not considered the waterproofing membrane of the roof system. Roof tiles serve three purposes: (1) they compliment the architectural design of the house, (2) they control the majority of the roof water by shedding water down their overlapping courses into a gutter or off the roof edge overhang, and (3) they protect the waterproofing membrane. The felt paper below the roof tiles, metal flashings, and the tiles themselves comprise the entire roof weatherproofing system. However, under extreme *out of the normal* weather conditions (i.e. wind-driven (horizontal) rains, snow or ice build-up), the roof system is more susceptible to water intrusion, especially on lower slope and flat roofs. Water intrusion may be unavoidable under extreme weather conditions.

Recommended Use and Maintenance:

- ✓ **NOTE**: **Do not walk on roof tiles**; concrete and clay tiles are subject to cracking and breaking. General inspections can be done from the ground, from ladders set at the edge of the roof, and from adjacent properties. Field glasses (binoculars) are often helpful. If more detailed inspections are necessary, it is advisable to hire a qualified, licensed and properly insured roof inspection contractor.

- ✓ Make periodic maintenance checks on the roof, including cleaning all drains, gutters and downspouts of leaves and other foreign debris, and checking all areas that have a caulking or sealant type material. The last category includes checking areas such as vents, pipe penetrations, sheet metal flashing and cracked sealant.

DO THIS......   NOT THIS!

INSPECTING THE ROOF

- ✓ You should be extremely careful when installing products on the roof (such as solar heaters) or fastening items to the roof (such as holiday lights). All aftermarket items attached to a roof should be made by a licensed contractor.

- ✓ The painting and caulking of flashings by a qualified roofing contractor is a routine maintenance item.

Appearance and Adhesion

Comments: Tiles generally become loose or slip where the roof meets a wall. Since tiles cannot be fastened with nails through sheet metal flashing, roofers may secure the tiles with roofing cement or other manufacturer recommended installation material. Loose tiles can slip off the roof and become a serious safety issue.

Recommended Use and Maintenance:

✓ Conduct periodic inspections along all roof-to-wall intersections and look for loose or slipping tiles. A preliminary assessment can most often be accomplished with a visual inspection from the ground or from an elevated portion of the structure. More complete inspections should be done only by qualified roofing specialists.

✓ Inspect the roof for any cracked or broken tiles within the first month of occupancy. Do not walk on the roof, do not make any roof penetrations, and do not fasten any objects to the roof. If you cannot inspect the roof with a ladder or by observation from a safe higher vantage point, hire a qualified roofing inspector to perform the job.

✓ You are responsible for keeping all sheet metal valleys, gutters and downspouts free from ice build-up, snow, leaves or other foreign debris *(see **Chapter 9 Miscellaneous, Ice and Snow**)*. This should be done safely from a ladder without walking on the roof or by a qualified roof maintenance service.

Composition Asphalt Shingles

Comments: Asphalt composition shingles are the water-shedding cover over the underlayment material of the roof system. Shingles serve two purposes: (1) to compliment the architectural design of the building, and (2) to control the majority of the roof water by shedding water down their overlapping courses and into a gutter or off the roof overhang edge. However, under extreme weather conditions (conditions *beyond the norm, such as horizontally driven rains*), and snow and ice build-up, the roof system is more susceptible to water intrusion, especially on low slope and flat roofs. Under extreme conditions, water intrusion may be unavoidable.

Recommended Use and Maintenance:

✓ Conduct periodic maintenance of the roof system. This includes cleaning all roof drains, gutters, valleys and downspouts of leaves and other foreign debris, checking areas that have a sealant material (i.e. vents and pipe penetrations), and inspecting all sheet metal flashing for deteriorated sealant.

✓ Avoid installing products or fastening items to or through the roof.

Appearance and Adhesion

Comments: Between the two types of asphalt shingles (organic and fiberglass), organic shingles have a history of curling and cupping, while some fiberglass shingles have a tendency to crack more easily than organic ones. Cupping and curling shingles can also be caused by inadequate attic ventilation.

Composition asphalt shingles may be covered in a grainy mineral surface. Loss of mineral granules from the shingle surface can occur as a result of 1) rooftop traffic (such as during installation of adjacent roofing materials or other building materials), 2) servicing of rooftop mounted heating and cooling equipment, and 3) natural weathering of the roof surface. Mineral granule loss can also be a result of poor ventilation or manufacturing defects. Minor loss of granules can be expected over the life span of the roof, and generally will not significantly impact the performance or life of the roof. However, excessive granule loss can cause premature breakdown of the membrane.

Recommended Use and Maintenance:

✓ As roofs age, particular attention should be paid to the condition of curled and cupped shingles. An occasional "tune-up" by a licensed and qualified roofing contractor can extend the life of the roof significantly.

✓ Do not permit excessive access to the roof. When access is required, adequate protection should be provided to the roof surface to prevent loss of mineral granules.

✓ Retain a qualified roofing professional to perform any addition or repair involving asphalt shingle roofs, hand-tabbing newly installed shingles, if necessary, to achieve proper seal to the underlying courses.

Wood Shake and Shingle Roofs

General Subject Information: Wood shakes and shingles have been traditional roof coverings (particularly in the West) for decades. Cedar is the primary wood used. The basic difference between a shingle and a shake is the thickness. Shakes are thicker and are often made by splitting cedar logs with a sharp tool similar to an ax. Additionally, both wood shakes and shingles can be manufactured by cutting the cedar log with a saw. Shakes are typically longer than shingles, and more of the shake is exposed to the weather. Unless they are chemically treated, wood shakes and shingles can pose a significant fire hazard, and some local jurisdictions have prohibited the installation of untreated shingles and shakes. Tile and composition shingles are gradually taking the place of wood shingles and shakes in homes.

Normal exposure to sunlight and rainfall results in loss of natural preservative oils from wood shakes and shingles and leads to some deformation of the wood. In addition, different rates of drying between the top and bottom surfaces of the shake or shingle can contribute to deformation of the wood. These are naturally occurring events and not generally a significant problem, other than an appearance issue.

Recommended Use and Maintenance:
✓ Gutters, downspouts and valleys should always be kept free of any leaves or other foreign debris.

✓ Any penetrations through the roof that exist should be carefully maintained with caulking, asphalt tar and roofing seals. Conduct a yearly inspection *prior to the winter season* to ensure that sheet metal caulking, sealant and asphalt cement have no cracks, voids or splits. The inspection and any required maintenance should be performed by a qualified, licensed and properly insured roofing contractor.

✓ Any after-market add-ons such as antennas, satellite dishes or solar collectors, may void the roof warranty. Consult with a licensed contractor and with the builder before making any changes or additions to the roof.

✓ Provide periodic maintenance in order to get a full useful life from a wood roof. Roof "tune-ups" from a licensed roofing contractor are recommended at a minimum of every five years. A "tune-up" can consist of replacing cupped or curled shakes and shingles, separating ridge caps, and blown off shingles. As compared to the cost of a new roof, a "tune-up" is not expensive and may easily extend the life of the roof.

✓ Special wood preservatives may be used to enhance and extend the life of such roofs. Older roofs that have not been maintained properly are likely to experience blow off of shakes and shingles.

✓ Accumulation of leaves, needles, dust sediment, and moss or fungi growth on wood shakes or shingles can lead to premature degradation of the wood. Periodic cleaning with a stiff bristle broom or low-pressure water spray can resolve most occurrences. DO NOT USE A POWER WASHER.

✓ Retain a qualified roofing professional to perform annual cleaning of the roof by removing accumulated growth of organic materials. Additionally, a regular application of moss or fungus inhibiting compounds, or the installation of moss or fungus inhibiting materials (such as zinc strips) can reduce the amount of growth. A roofing professional should be consulted for product and application information.

Composite or Synthetic Roof System

General Subject Information: Numerous composite or synthetic materials are now available for steep-sloped water shedding roofs. These products are engineered and manufactured to simulate the appearance of natural materials (such as wood shakes, shingles, slate or tile), while providing wind uplift and fire resistance. These products include: fiber cement composites, formed metal panels, foil-laminate asphalt shingles, wood fiber based materials, fiberglass and polymer based products, and various recycled materials. Many of these products and their respective installation methods are continually changing. The manufacturer's design and installation recommendations should be consulted for information regarding proper design, installation and maintenance of these products.

Recommended Use and Maintenance:
✓ You should conduct a thorough inspection of the roof at the time of the *walkthrough*.
✓ Do not walk on the roof, make any penetrations through, or fasten any item to the roof.
✓ Retain a qualified roofing professional on an annual schedule to perform inspections of the roof, noting and replacing any cracked or broken materials, and noting and securing any materials found to be loose or displaced.
✓ Conduct a yearly inspection (*prior to the winter season*) to ensure that sheet metal caulking, sealant or asphalt cement are not damaged by cracks, voids or splits. The inspection, and any required maintenance, should be performed by a qualified, licensed and properly insured roofing professional.

Roof Ventilation

General Subject Information: Proper ventilation helps dissipate and reduce unwanted moisture in the attic during the winter and hot air during the summer. Vents located low on the roof system help bring in cooler air, while vents located closer to or on the *ridge* help remove warm or moist air.

Comments: It is considered normal if water penetrates through the vent or louver during extreme weather conditions for the geographical region.

Recommended Use and Maintenance:
✓ Keep all vents and louvers free from any obstructions. Do not allow birds to nest in vents.
✓ Inspect vents annually to ensure the screens in the vents are intact. Loose or torn screens are an invitation for bees and other insects.

KEEPING GUTTERS CLEAN - **BEFORE** THE RAINY SEASON

Eaves

General Subject Information: The "*eave*" is a part of the roof that generally hangs out past the exterior walls. Gutters are often applied directly to the *fascia* board of the eaves. Eaves help protect the house by preventing rain from coming directly down the face of the walls, and by reducing direct sunlight into the residence that can damage interior finishes and furnishings. Eaves are generally not the cause of damage to interior finishes or furnishings. However, ice build-up from *ice dams* or water blockage from *clogged gutters and valleys,* can allow water to back up the roof, migrate under the felt (*underlayment*) and cause interior roof damage.

Recommended Use and Maintenance:
- ✓ Provide proper maintenance to the eaves and surrounding roof components. This includes keeping gutters free from debris and clearing ice dams that may develop.
- ✓ Maintain the eaves with a regular schedule of inspection followed by any necessary painting, caulking and removal of any debris that might constrict the flow of water. This includes annual gutter cleaning.

Built Up Roofing and Other Low Slope Roofs

General Subject Information: A built up roof (**BUR**) system is simply layers of asphalt that serve as the waterproofing medium which are sandwiched between various types of roofing membranes known as felts. Even though in residential construction BUR systems are not as common as other roofing materials, they are found where low *slope* or flat roof conditions exist. From entry level homes to condominium buildings to expensive desert homes, built up roofs often achieve a particular look that the architect is trying establish. There are actually three basic types of BUR that are used today: smooth surface, aggregate surface and mineral surface.

Another type of low slope roof system is the single-ply roof. This system consists of a single membrane layer that is applied with fasteners over the *underlayment* (also called a substrate). The seams are sealed with a special sealant provided by the manufacturer.

Voids between two waterproof layers of roofing materials can cause bubbles or blisters. When moist air gets trapped between these two layers, the rise in temperature increases the pressure between the two layers and may cause them to be pushed apart. Nearly all roofs may experience some bubbles and blisters. If the bubbles and blisters are unbroken and under 12 inches in diameter, they should be left alone. Puncturing and attempting to repair the unbroken blisters can result in leaks.

It is important that the roofing manufacturer's installation recommendations are closely followed both for the life of the roof and to comply with any warranty by the manufacturer. Finally, the homeowner should provide preventive maintenance to the roof, as the life span may be greatly influenced by the presence or absence of proper roof maintenance.

Recommended Use and Maintenance:
- ✓ This type of roof system needs an annual inspection and maintenance program. At a minimum, this should entail clearing debris that could damage the roof membrane, sealing any cracks, tears or rips, and keeping drains, gutters and downspouts free from debris. Gravel or mineral has a tendency to clog drains and fill gutters. Always check the roof prior to and after any inclement weather or winter rains.

✔ Retain a qualified roofing professional to perform annual roof inspections. Note and repair any anomalies that are found, such as backed out fasteners.

✔ Pay special attention to areas where the roof turns up to a wall or skylight since the felt material is susceptible to deterioration and may produce leaks if not properly maintained.

✔ If the roof has **parapet** walls, then all overflow **scuppers** or primary and secondary drains must be kept free of leaves, gravel, and debris.

✔ Aftermarket products such as deck boards, satellite dishes and solar panels should not be fastened directly to the roof system without consulting the builder or a licensed roofing contractor.

✔ As a general rule, avoid walking on the roof. To protect the roof membrane from splitting or tearing, steer clear from excessive roof foot traffic, including the areas where materials transition from the horizontal to the vertical.

✔ As the roof begins to age, you will need to provide periodic maintenance to joints and separations. Areas that have received tar or caulking materials will also need periodic maintenance due to age and structure movement. Pay particular attention to locations where dissimilar materials meet (i.e., plumbing vents or metal flashing). The joining of dissimilar materials is a prime location for water intrusion, especially as tar and caulking become more brittle and crack.

Chapter Five

EXTERIOR COMPONENTS

includes:

Walkways and Driveways

Garage Doors

Decks and Patios

Windows and Patio Doors

French Doors/Other Exterior Doors
Door Hardware

Chimneys and Flues

Gutters, Downspouts and Flashing

Skylights

Paint and Stain

Exterior Components

Walkways and Driveways

General Subject Information: When it comes to concrete, there is one fact that all homeowners, builders, and tradespersons must realize: CONCRETE WILL CRACK. Concrete walkways and driveways are constructed with joints that create a weakened plane or thinner section of concrete. The purpose of these control joints is to control and contain the cracking to specific areas. Therefore, cracks in control joints are a common occurrence and are considered normal. The degree to which concrete cracks or the deviation in vertical displacement are the criteria used to determine if the cracking is unacceptable or within industry standards. There are many reasons that concrete products crack and most are not related to any structural problems.

Comments: When trees are planted in the vicinity of any concrete work, there is the potential for the root system to undermine the concrete and cause it to eventually crack, heave and settle (this holds true for the foundation as well). If the driveway is used for large RV storage, it may crack due to the weight of the RV. RVs should be stored on a separate concrete and steel reinforced pad that is at least 6-inches thick. Moving vans should be parked on the street. Concrete trucks used by aftermarket contractors for pools and patios should be parked on the street, and their contents should be pumped to the desired location.

Generally speaking, the further away from the foundation, the less compaction there is within the soils. Concrete sidewalks are much more susceptible to heaving or subsiding than a structural foundation. Not only is the soil potentially not as well compacted, but there may be a flow of irrigation water to the landscape. If the soils are high in clay content, water will cause the soils to expand; when the soils dry out they start to contract. Both expansion and contraction apply an excessive amount of stress upon concrete.

Recommended Use and Maintenance:

✓ Cracks that occur at **control joints** are a routine homeowner maintenance item. This maintenance consists of filling the crack with a suitable concrete caulk.

✓ Also maintain the area around the driveway in a way that will not allow soils to be washed away from beneath the driveway.

THIS TREE WAS PLANTED TOO CLOSE TO THE SIDEWALK... ITS ROOTS PUSHED UP THE WALK!

✓ Tree roots are a primary cause for concrete to heave and crack in landscaped areas. When placing trees in the vicinity of any concrete product, it is important to consider the potential growth of the root system (for example, palm trees have very small root balls, while the root system of a willow is extensive and will cause significant heaving of drives and walks). Seek the advice of a licensed landscape architect or contractor and install a root barrier system in these instances.

✓ You should take care not to overwater surrounding areas, as this can lead to expansion of soils.

✓ Be careful not to alter the original site drainage.

✓ Do not let any irrigation undermine the sidewalks. Sidewalks need to have a very solid foundation in order to prevent any cracking or damage from occurring.

Appearance and Miscellaneous

Comments: During design and engineering of the site, the streets and lots are calculated to provide positive water drainage away from streets and residences. These designs are fairly standard, and they take into consideration wheelbase and clearance of most vehicles. However, vehicles with exceptionally long or short wheelbases or vehicles that have been lowered are likely to scrape or bottom out.

Concrete is a material that can be susceptible to *spalling*, scaling, or chipping. Use of certain materials by homeowners can lead to this condition. See Recommended Use and Maintenance below.

Concrete may sometimes appear blotchy or mottled in color. Concrete often dries, or cures, in a non-uniform manner. This causes the difference in appearance. Usually within two years, concrete color becomes more uniform as the surface of the concrete reacts to the air. Refer to Recommended Use and Maintenance below for additional information.

Recommended Use and Maintenance:
✓ Do not spill acidic products or create excessive landscape moisture that may cause damage to the concrete surface. If you use rock salt as an ice-removing agent, you assume the risk of damage to the concrete (and surrounding landscape as well).

✓ The concrete steps or stoops that join to the foundation may have separations. This is usually the result of the foundation and stoops settling at different rates. Separations measuring up to ¼-inch should be maintained with concrete caulk to fill the gap.

✓ If the non-uniform color of concrete is bothersome, brush the darker areas with a wire broom. This will allow air to reach the darker areas, and equalize the color at a faster rate.

Garage Doors

Comments: Most garage door performance is related to proper care and maintenance by the homeowner. Occasionally, garage doors equipped with an automatic opener may mysteriously open and close. The transmitter may share a radio frequency with other devices, such as another garage transmitter in the neighborhood, or an airplane flying overhead. Signals from these transmitters will activate the automatic door opener. Most openers have programmable code switches that can be changed if this condition occurs.

Recommended Use and Maintenance:

- ✓ Maintain and protect the garage door as necessary. Inadequate maintenance or misuse can result in poor performance of the garage door. Damage to the door, frame, and guides that results in poor performance of the door is your responsibility. Proper lubrication of the door tracks and operating mechanism is discussed in the **Homeowner Maintenance Summary, Garage Doors**.
- ✓ Maintain garage doors in accordance with the manufacturer's recommendations and avoid abusive or negligent use of doors that could result in damage.
- ✓ One-piece garage doors may sag with age and should be lubricated at the hinge points every six months with 30w oil. The keepers (the long threaded rods that run across the top and bottom) should be kept tight to prevent the door from sagging in the middle.
- ✓ Sectional doors (doors that roll up into the garage ceiling on tracks) should have the track rollers lubricated with 30w oil annually.
- ✓ The automatic openers; whether they are chain drive, screw drive or belt drive, should have the drive mechanism annually lubricated with a light grease. (Some belt drive mechanisms may not need to be lubricated – be sure to read the owner's manual.)
- ✓ Garage doors vibrate while opening and closing. It is important that an inspection be made every six months for the first year and annually thereafter, for bolts that can be wiggled or moved by hand.
- ✓ Read and follow the instruction manual that is furnished with the automatic door opener.

Decks and Patios

General Subject Information: Decks and patios are accessory structures used to enhance the architecture and livability of the house. Most decks and patios are installed by an aftermarket contractor or the owner. In the case of a planned community such as a condominium or townhouse project, the decks and patios are typically installed as part of original construction.

Because decks are exposed continually to weather, they require more maintenance and have a shorter useful life than other exterior components. Apart from original construction, the useful life of a deck and patio will depend upon the degree of maintenance, the annual rainfall in the area, local weather conditions, and which direction the deck or patio faces.

Recommended Use and Maintenance:

- ✓ Keep decks clean and free of dirt and debris so that they will not become slippery or plug the deck drains during storms.
- ✓ If deck drains are installed, they should be flushed with a garden hose prior to the start of the rainy season and periodically during the rainy season. Overflow drains should be inspected to ensure that they are not clogged with leaves or other debris.
- ✓ Potted plants should not be placed directly

DEBRIS SHOULD COME OUT THE OTHER END OF THE PIPE

FLUSH YARD AND DRIVEWAY DRAINS **BEFORE** THE RAINS BEGIN

on the deck surface. They should be placed on stands or spacers to allow air to circulate underneath. Plant stands with metal legs should be avoided. If used, steps must be taken to protect the deck surface from penetration by the metal legs.

Appearance and Miscellaneous

Comments:
Concrete decks and patios, whether natural in color or whether colored by adding agents to the mix, are not likely to dry (cure) in a uniform manner. Many factors influence the surface appearance of concrete that is less than a year old. Factors include the amount of moisture in the underlying soil and the humidity during the first 30 days. The more moisture in the soil and air, the greater the chances for non-uniform surface color. Over time (usually within 2 years) the non-uniform color will gradually become uniform as the surface of the concrete reacts to the air. Wood decks typically require annual maintenance.

Recommended Use and Maintenance:
- ✓ Perform an annual inspection of the deck and renail all loose boards and raised nails.
- ✓ Recoat the top boards with a good quality deck sealer every one or two years, depending upon the amount of exposure. Deck sealers with pigment last longer than clear sealers.
- ✓ Keep the underside of the deck free of debris and storage materials so that air can circulate underneath.
- ✓ The surface of soil should be kept at least 8 inches below the bottom of wood posts.
- ✓ Landscape shrubs should not be allowed to grow around posts as moisture may cause dryrot to the posts.
- ✓ After the walkthrough, renailing or screw tightening of deck boards is your maintenance item. Deck boards shrink as they dry out, and they also move up and down with seasonal temperature changes.
- ✓ If the deck has wooden railings, the rail post bolts should be tightened every 6 months during the first two years of occupancy as a safety precaution.
- ✓ Maintain all drainage courses and catch basins so that they are free of dirt, leaves and other debris. Do not place unreasonably heavy loads on deck surfaces such as tree sized potted plants.
- ✓ If you want to speed up the process of equalizing the color of a concrete deck, you can brush the concrete with a wire broom and allow the air to react with the darker areas.

Windows and Patio Doors

General Subject Information: Windows come in many different types such as side vent, single hung, double hung, and fixed. Patio doors are, for industry purposes, considered a large window. Both window and patio door frames are made of metal (usually aluminum), wood, or plastic (PVC), or a combination of these materials. The installation methods and operation of windows and patio doors are similar. The purpose of this section is to cover suggested maintenance for windows and patio doors.

Comments: Most windows and patio doors installed in houses are *dual pane* glass (two panes of glass made into a "sandwich" with dead air space in the middle). The "sandwich" is sealed so the air cannot enter or leave the space. This dead air space provides an insulating quality that single pane windows do not have. When the seal is broken, moisture enters between the panes and the window becomes foggy. Seal materials have greatly improved in recent years, allowing manufacturers to extend their warranties.

Wind-driven rain can sometimes penetrate window weather seals and joints. Wind-driven rain can also blow back through the weep holes into the interior of the house. Windows should be selected in accordance with the American Architectural Manufacturer's Association (AAMA) "R"-ratings that match window systems with weather conditions found in the home's geographic location. It must be noted that even a properly selected window can leak if exposed to extreme wind or rain. During a storm it is not unusual to find that the sill track of the window is filled with water. At the conclusion of the inclement weather (wind and rain), the water will drain out of the track if the weep holes are kept open and free of debris.

Recommended Use and Maintenance:

FIRST, CLEAN JOINT...
THEN APPLY CAULKING

INSPECT AND CAULK TRIM ANNUALLY

✔ Take care to inspect all windows and patio doors prior to delivery of your home, especially if your home has a stucco finish. Sand from the stucco may find its way onto the glass, and window washers can accidentally make small scratches in the glass when they are trying to clean it.

✔ Never use an abrasive cleaner on glass.

✔ Doors and windows have a tendency to "stick" during the winter months because the wood frame of the house absorbs moisture and expands slightly. Lubricate the rollers and slides with an approved window lubricant (available at any hardware store) and adjust the rollers on the patio doors as routine maintenance items.

✔ Patio sliding doors should have their tracks (bottom sill) swept and vacuumed monthly. The weep holes should also be inspected and cleaned as needed. Dust and dirt build-up in slider door tracks will interfere with the proper operation of the small wheels that the doors slide on. For swing doors, the hinges and latches should be lubricated annually with a dry lubricant specifically made for locks and latches.

✔ Inspect for broken or breached window seals in dual or triple pane windows. Breached window seals greatly diminish the window's insulating value.

✔ Do not tint the inside of a dual pane window. The resulting excessive heat build up between the panes of glass can rupture the seals. *Refer to **Ten Most Common Mistakes Made By Homeowners** located in the Introduction.*

✔ Perform an annual inspection of all windows and doors, clean debris from all window and patio door weep holes, and caulk all inside corners of the sill. This maintenance is especially important in geographic areas that have trees with small leaves and also areas that experience dust storms. *Refer to **Ten Most Common Mistakes Made By Homeowners** located in the Introduction.*

French Doors and Other Exterior Doors

General Subject Information: "French" style doors are becoming popular in homes today. Other exterior doors include the front door, rear door and garage pedestrian door. Patio doors, which are actually considered a specialty window, are covered in the "Windows and Patio Doors" Section of this Chapter. Generally, if doors open (swing) into the house, they offer a better degree of weather protection.

Comments: Manufacturers of exterior doors generally provide specific installation and maintenance recommendations. These recommendations should be adhered to strictly.

Recommended Use and Maintenance:

✓ The weep holes at the bottom of windows and patio doors serve a purpose: to allow water to drain out from the track during rainstorms. Weep holes should be inspected annually to make sure that no accumulated debris is obstructing drainage pathways.

✓ If exterior door trim and joints between the door frame and the exterior wall surface are caulked, inspect caulking annually and re-caulk (including the threshold) as necessary to maintain a weather-tight seal.

✓ Keep doors closed during wet weather.

✓ Depending upon geographic location and exposure, the weatherstrips at the doors will need to be replaced every three to five years.

✓ Do not place any load on door *leaves*, as they are not designed for this purpose and may sag over time. Keep door leaves and frames in good condition by repainting and re-caulking on a periodic basis. Adhere to the manufacturer's recommendations.

✓ Sometimes it is necessary to correct the fit of wood doors, either because of minor swelling or because surrounding finishes were replaced with materials of different thickness (for example, floor coverings). Any corrections should be done professionally, and any bare wood should be immediately and completely sealed. If the bottom of a door is cut due to a change in flooring material, the fresh cut should be sealed.

✓ The door bottom weather stripping should be checked in the first year to see that it seals the threshold and there are no large gaps where daylight can be seen. If there is a large gap, lower the door weather strip by loosening the four or five screws at the bottom strip and pull the strip down so it seals uniformly across the threshold.

✓ Both door and window weather stripping will wear out over time. The condition of weather stripping should be inspected annually. Depending upon use, weather stripping should be replaced every five to ten years.

Hardware

Comments: Hardware exposed to outdoor conditions requires special attention, both in selection and maintenance. The fact that an item of hardware is corrosion-resistant does not mean that it will not become discolored. For example, bright brass hardware, which is commonly used in exterior applications, has a factory-applied lacquer coating. Homeowners are often not aware of this, and when the lacquer finish eventually breaks down (as it almost certainly will) dark spots will appear. The homeowner may then conclude that the product is unacceptable and this is not the case. Proper maintenance at this time will restore the finish, but more frequent care will be required thereafter. It is advisable to wait for 2 days after applying varnish, paint, or stain to a door before installing brass hardware to avoid chemical reactions between the brass and the curing finish that could cause staining.

Recommended Use and Maintenance:
- ✓ First, make sure to read the manufacturer's maintenance and care recommendations.
- ✓ Keep hardware clean and bright by polishing on a regular basis with a clean, soft cloth. Do not allow dust and other deleterious materials to accumulate.
- ✓ To preserve the factory-applied coating, avoid any abrasive products such as cleaners or polishing pads.
- ✓ While good care will extend the life of brass coatings, they will eventually break down and dark spots may appear. When tarnish reaches an undesirable level, the hardware should be removed from the door and the remaining lacquer coating completely removed. Coating removal should be done in accordance with the manufacturer's recommendations.

Chimneys and Flues

General Subject Information: The vast majority of fireplaces and flues that are installed in homes are metal factory-built assemblies. The traditional masonry fireplace and chimney is now relegated to custom home construction. Factory-built assemblies will provide good service if properly used and maintained. With the environmental regulations on air quality getting tougher every year, the wood burning fireplace may become a thing of the past. See **Chapter 6 "Fireplaces"** for further information.

Recommended Use and Maintenance:

- ✓ And all-fuel chimney flue should be professionally cleaned every two years if there are more than 50 wood fires per year or if there are more than 25 fires per year using manufactured fore logs made of wax and sawdust, subject to any restrictions or requirements of the manufacturer.
- ✓ You should schedule an inspection of the chimney cap and flue termination after having burned two cords of wood. Wood with a high pitch content, such as pine, will cause combustion deposits to accumulate in the flue faster and require more frequent inspections.
- ✓ If the original installation secured the chimney cap through the horizontal surface of the chase cover, periodically check the caulking of the attachment screws to avoid water penetration.
- ✓ See **Chapter 6 "Fireplaces"** for recommendations regarding cleaning of the flue. Dirty flues can cause poorly drawing fireplaces.
- ✓ Also, overloading the fireplace with too much fuel may cause both smoke and fire to enter the room. Never burn newspapers or gift wrappings.
- ✓ If glass doors are installed as part of the fireplace, they must be closed during burning operation. Fireplaces that do not have glass doors should not have them added unless specifically approved by the manufacturer.

Gutters and Downspouts

General Subject Information: During the dry summer months, it is easy to forget the effects of a hard rain. Control of rainwater from roofs is important for the long-term performance of houses. Significant amounts of water can flow over the edge of a sloped roof during a strong rainstorm. If uncontrolled, this water will flow down wall surfaces and increase the likelihood of leaks at windows, doors and through wall surface coverings. When water from the roof hits the ground next to a house, water and soil can splash onto the lower surfaces of the structure. This may produce unsightly and potentially damaging conditions. Gutters are the best way to control water flow from eaves. Downspouts direct water from the gutters to the ground in a controlled manner. If installed, downspouts and gutters should be sized according to the Sheet Metal and Air Conditioning Contractors' National Association (SMACNA) guidelines or with International Plumbing Code design criteria.

Recommended Use and Maintenance:

FAILURE TO KEEP GUTTERS CLEAN CAN RESULT IN RUSTING AND LEAKING!

- ✓ Keep gutters free of leaves, toys and other debris. The slope of a level gutter can easily be adversely reversed by allowing debris to accumulate. Further, the acid produced by decaying leaves or bird droppings will, over time, eat through a metal gutter. Gutters should be cleaned annually and more frequently if mature trees are adjacent to the house.
- ✓ If the house is in an area with mature trees, it is a good idea to place gutter screens along the gutter length and in the top opening of each downspout to help minimize leaf debris. Prune branches that overhang roofs and gutters.
- ✓ If a gutter or downspout leaks, have it repaired at the first opportunity.
- ✓ If gutters are made of galvanized sheet metal (as opposed to aluminum or plastic), their life will be greatly reduced if you allow acidic bird droppings, eucalyptus leaves or pine needles to accumulate in the gutter.
- ✓ To prevent storm water from accumulating near the foundation, do not alter the finished grades around the house that were provided upon delivery of the house to you. Any change to the finished grade should be done according to Code and as directed by a licensed landscape architect or civil engineer.
- ✓ Keep all drainage swales free of debris. Flush out the underground pipe system with a garden hose prior to the start of the rainy season.
- ✓ If downspout noise exists to the extent and in a location that affects the quality of habitability (such as outside a bedroom window) the following suggestions can mitigate the noise:
  - → If the bottom of downspout is "kicked out" from the wall and is not inserted into a collection pipe, glue a piece of carpet padding into the kicked out portion. Make sure the metal is clean and dry and use a watertight glue. Inspect the discharge during the rainy season to keep it cleared of any leaves or debris.
  - → If the downspout has several twists and turns and the bottom is not accessible, hang a galvanized steel or plastic chain with one inch wide links into the top 3 to 5 feet of the downspout. Hang the top link from a copper or brass rod that is at least 12 inches long. It is important that the chain and the rod be made of a material that does not rust. Inspect the chain frequently during the rainy season and clean it as necessary.

Skylights

General Subject Information: Skylights are simply windows in the roof. Like windows, skylights can either be fixed (cannot open) or operable (can open). The most commonly used skylights are made of acrylic or similar plastics, usually shaped in the form of a dome and set in an aluminum frame. Some skylights have flat plate glass in them. Another type of skylight is in the form of a tube that directs light through attics into a light diffuser at the level of the ceiling.

Recommended Use and Maintenance:
- ✓ Be aware of the amount of humidity created in kitchens, baths, laundry rooms and other areas or devices that produce water vapor. This may result in excessive condensation at skylights. Fans should always be operating while these rooms are in use to reduce humidity.
- ✓ Do not tint the inside surface of a dual pane skylight, as the heat may cause the seal to fail.
- ✓ If a particular skylight warms the room too much and you feel uncomfortable with performance of the skylight, there are several screening and shading techniques and products available to provide additional protection.

Paint and Stain

General Subject Information: Simply defined, stains are liquids that penetrate into the surface (usually wood) allowing the *grain* to be visible, while paints cover the surface of the material thus making the material invisible. Stains can be clear (without pigment) or semi-transparent (with some pigment). For the most part, stains do not last as long as paint. Correct preparation of surfaces to receive paints and stains, and the selection of an appropriate product for the use intended are essential in achieving a satisfactory finish. Adequate homeowner maintenance and refinishing at suitable intervals are equally important. The durability of painted and stained surfaces is also directly related to the exposure to which it is subjected. Surfaces that receive direct sun or the full force of storms can be expected to require more frequent refinishing. The first coat of paint, the one applied during construction, is the coat that will last the shortest time, as the material beneath the paint absorbs a much greater percentage of the first coat of paint than successive coats.

Comments: Some types and colors of paints are more susceptible to fading and chalking when exposed to direct sunlight. For example, dark colors are more prone to fading than lighter colors. Manufacturers can provide useful guidance for selection of paints that will perform effectively under particular climactic conditions.

Recommended Use and Maintenance:
- ✓ It is important to observe the condition of painted surfaces on a periodic basis. There is no standard schedule for exterior paint or stain reapplication. It is the homeowner's responsibility to be vigilant and observe all wear and tear of paint and stain. An annual inspection is recommended. Paints first begin to show signs of wear in limited areas. Maintain paint surfaces in a clean and well-ventilated condition. Touch up any areas at the first sign of premature aging or deterioration. This can significantly extend the life of the overall paint job.
- ✓ Periodically inspect exterior surfaces to determine if mildew or fungus growth is occurring. Any growth of these organisms should be addressed by proper cleaning and application of products that will kill the organisms and retard their return. This should be done promptly

upon observation of mildews or fungi, because once established, these organisms are progressively more difficult to control and eradicate. If you observe significant condensation on exterior surfaces (usually at windows and cool exterior walls), an effort should be made to find the right balance of natural and mechanical ventilation to minimize the problem.

✓ At interior locations, always use the mechanical ventilation in bathrooms, laundry rooms, and kitchens while these rooms are in use, and regularly air out rooms that have windows.

✓ Bathroom and laundry fans should be vacuumed with a hose vacuum and crevice tool at least once a year.

✓ Keep all varnished and lacquered surfaces reasonably free of excessive moisture, heat, dust and from other damaging conditions. Relatively frequent maintenance and recoating with a high quality marine spar varnish should be part of routine maintenance.

✓ Keep stained surfaces clean and free of debris. Adequate ventilation of exposed surfaces should be provided. You should recoat stained surfaces at an interval no longer than that which is recommended by the paint or stain manufacturer or when surface deterioration is first observed.

MOIST AIR PASSES THROUGH THE BATHROOM FAN

DO THIS...

OR THIS

MOIST AIR GOES OUT AN OPEN WINDOW

REDUCE THE CHANCES OF MOLD GROWTH WHEN SHOWERING.

Special Section on Exterior Paints and Coatings

Lap Siding or Panel Siding with Wood Trim:

Whether the house has hardboard siding, cement board siding or panel siding, it probably has wood trim around the windows and doors. It may have wood trim elsewhere too, such as a horizontal trim band between the first and second floors, or trim boards over the butt joints of the panels.

✓ The trim is likely to be the first to show the effects of weathering, ahead of the lap boards or panels themselves. Caulking and painting of the trim is probably going to be needed in the second or third year, particularly on south and west exposures. Replace any trim that has warped more than ¼ inch. Avoid trying to fill gaps with caulk that are in excess of ¼ inch.

✓ Wood panel siding is next in line for timing of repainting. Thin spots in the paint will appear and small cracks in the surface of the wood will begin to show. This condition usually occurs in the third or fourth year of the life of the house.

✓ Next in the time schedule for painting is the lap siding. The body of the painted surfaces will show a thinning, and the butt joints will show some separations. This condition usually occurs in the fourth or fifth year of the life of the house.

✓ When repainting the trim, it is recommended to use a high quality semi-gloss or eggshell finish, rather than a flat finish. The semi-gloss or eggshell surfaces generally stand up to the weather better and they are easier to keep clean.

✓ When repainting the body, it is recommended to use the top of the line grade from a reputable paint manufacturer. Since the labor to apply the paint is the same as that of a lesser grade, the extra cost for the top grade is worth not having to repaint as often.

Stucco (with or without wood trim):

The house may have a three coat stucco cladding, or it may have a one or two coat system. The exterior surface may be painted, or it may be color-coated. Color coating is a process where a colored pigment is added to the final coat of stucco before it is applied. The advantage to color coating is that a separate operation (painting) is not necessary; the disadvantage is that color coated surfaces are extremely hard to re-color a small area without re-coloring the entire exterior.

✓ If the stucco has wood trim around the windows and doors, treat the maintenance the same as the wood trim described above in the siding section.

✓ If the stucco has been painted, repainting will probably be needed in the fifth year of the life of the house. Be sure to use a paint that is made by a reputable paint manufacturer and specifically formulated for exterior stucco. Do not use elastomeric paint—it will seal the pores in the stucco and can cause moisture to remain in the wall cavity. Elastomeric paint is sold as a solution for hiding minor stucco cracks, but its main drawback is that it prevents the stucco from "breathing".

✓ If the stucco is color coated (you can tell by chipping off a small piece in an area not normally visible, and see if the color runs clear through the chip), it is recommended that the stucco be repainted rather than re-color coated. Painted stucco is easier to touch up than colored stucco. Again, refer to the warning about elastomeric paint in the paragraph above.

✓ Stucco cracks. When the time comes to repaint the stucco, it is also time to repair the cosmetic (non-structural) cracks too. The best stucco crack repair material is stucco itself that is forced into the cracks using a mason's sponge backed float. Products that are sold as stucco crack fillers have a plastic material in them that does not absorb paint (or color) at the same rate as virgin stucco. Consequently, the cracks often "reflect" through the newly painted surface and are more prominent than the unfilled cracks.

Chapter Six

INTERIOR
COMPONENTS

includes:

Fireplaces

Insulation

Interior Doors and Door Hardware

Finish Flooring:
**Hardwood, Ceramic Tile and Clay,
Marble, Granite, Stone,
Vinyl and Carpet Floors**

Plaster and Drywall

Countertops

Appliances

Cabinets and Vanities

Moldings and Trim

Mirrors, Shower and Tub Enclosures

nterior Components

Fireplaces

General Subject Information: Fireplaces that are installed in houses today function more as decorative items than as sources of heat. Many fireplaces are considered gas appliances and are not equipped to burn anything other than the gas supplied to them. A wood burning fireplace operating without its glass doors closed will actually draw more heat from the room than it gives back to the room. Refer to **Chapter Five "Chimneys and Flues"** for additional information.

Comments: A typical chimney built today will be capped with a code-approved *spark arrestor* usually underneath a metal bonnet. A few fireplaces are still being constructed with a masonry *flue*. These chimneys will have a spark arrestor, but they may not have a metal, stucco or concrete cap. Because all chimneys must be open to the outside in order to perform, they may pass some rainwater during periods of extreme wind-driven rain.

Recommended Use and Maintenance:

✓ Keep the *damper* closed when the fireplace is not in use. Note: If the fireplace is used for burning wood, be certain there are no live coals or embers before closing the damper. Otherwise, poisonous gases could enter the room.

✓ The flue must be cleaned (swept) periodically from the top, going downward, in accordance with the manufacturer's instructions and according to the amount of use of the fireplace. This is a dirty job that is best left to professional chimney sweeps. Failure to keep the chimney clean can result in dangerous flue fires high up in the chimney.

✓ Always be sure the damper is open before starting a fire. Do not overload the firebox with too much fuel or improper fuel (such as holiday gift wrappings). Use only the fuel that is approved by the manufacturer (a gas log fireplace is typically not suited to burn wood or paper).

✓ If installed, glass doors should be closed during fireplace operation.

✓ You should "cure" new refractory panels by building a series of small, low-heat fires before fully using the entire fireplace. It is important to read the owner's instruction manual and avoid creating high heat fires with items such as wrapping paper, composition logs or lumber.

DO NOT BURN WRAPPING PAPER!

USE THE CORRECT FUEL FOR THE FIRE PLACE IN YOUR HOUSE

✓ Always place logs into the firebox using metal tongs; logs thrown into the firebox may hit the refractory and crack it. Avoid burning any composite wood material such as particle board or glulam beam scraps.

✓ Dampers will become rusty because water is formed when any type of fuel is burned. It is normal to expect some rust on the damper and its hinges. If the damper becomes difficult to operate, the hinges can be sprayed with a rust removing lubricant. <u>WARNING</u>: Do not spray when there is a fire or hot coals present. The spray may be flammable.

Insulation

<u>General Subject Information:</u> Insulation is important for house comfort and decreased dependency on energy usage. In a new homes, insulation is required as part of the issuance of a building permit. Because government requirements deal with energy consumption, it is important to note that insulation is just one of the components of proper energy conservation. Other components include efficient furnaces, water heaters, window glazing, air conditioning and *weatherstripping*. For example, it is possible to have more insulation and a less efficient furnace as long as the energy value calculation of the entire house meets the requirements.

Insulation comes in two forms: (1) batts, often made of fiberglass and are pink or yellow in color and 15 or 23 inches wide by 8 or 10 feet long, and (2) loose fill, which looks like packing material, and is generally blown through a large hose into the attic space.

<u>Comments:</u> Much of the comfort a house provides depends on the lifestyle of the occupants. For example, it is unrealistic to expect that an air conditioner turned on at 5 pm on a hot summer day can effectively and entirely cool the house by bedtime. Refer to **Chapter Seven, "Cooling"**.

<u>Recommended Use and Maintenance:</u>

✓ In wintertime furnaces should be programmed to come on in the morning at least 30 minutes before the time occupants wake. Constant adjustments to the thermostat will result in uneven temperatures and periods of discomfort.

✓ Installation of insulating drapes and shades is an important way to increase house comfort and decrease energy consumption.

✓ If you want to decrease energy consumption, adding insulation to the attic is the most effective way to achieve energy savings. If additional attic insulation is installed, care should be taken not to block the eave vents or allow the material to touch vents from gas fired appliances.

✓ When adding or replacing appliances, always install ones that have the Energy Star™ rating.

Interior Doors

<u>Comments:</u> With the exception of a small number of custom homes, most doors are manufactured as completed assemblies, consisting of the door hung with hinges in the *jamb*. Door manufacturers routinely hold the bottom of the door up to 1-3/8 inches from the bottom of the jamb when building the door assembly. This allows for a variety of finish floor coverings of different thickness, such as wood, carpet, tile and vinyl (resilient flooring).

Recommended Use and Maintenance:

✔ Do not hang anything heavy on doors or doorknobs. This can pull the top hinges out of adjustment and negatively affect the door swing. This can also negatively affect the ability of the latch to engage.

✔ Seasonal humidity changes can result in temporarily impaired door swing performance; this is normal.

✔ Operate the doors, including *pocket doors*, in a normal fashion and do not slam the doors back and forth.

✔ You can expect a larger gap between the bottom of the door and the top of the floor surface in a room that has vinyl flooring (like a laundry room) than in a room that has carpet flooring.

Door Hardware

Comments: The finish life of doorknobs and levers depends on finish type, location, and amount of use. Bright brass finishes are most susceptible to tarnishing. Oil from palms of hands and finger rings will contribute to the tarnishing process. Air pollution also contributes to the tarnishing process.

Recommended Use and Maintenance:

✔ Door latch mechanisms should be lubricated annually with a dry lubricant made specifically for that use.

✔ Learn about the proper care of metal finishes, especially bright brass, and conduct appropriate maintenance for the particular metal finish. If the house is located in a marine environment, expect pitting and tarnishing of the hardware finishes unless the hardware is labeled "lifetime finished".

✔ Refer to the manufacturer's warranty and maintenance requirements.

Closets

Recommended Use and Maintenance:

✔ Do not overload closet poles with heavy clothing or with too much clothing. This will cause poles to deflect, crack, or pull out of *rosettes*.

✔ In regions of high humidity, it is wise to leave closet doors partially open so that air can circulate and reduce the chances of clothes becoming mildewed.

Finish Flooring

General Subject Information: Finish flooring is the final surface to be applied to the *subfloor*. This product may be carpet, hardwood, ceramic tile, marble, or resilient flooring (vinyl). Care and use varies with each type of flooring. Some products are more vulnerable to water spills, scratching, and foot traffic than others.

Recommended Use and Maintenance:

✓ Examine all finish floors carefully at the time of your walkthrough.

✓ Maintain flooring using products and methods approved by the manufacturer or trade association whose products have been installed.

✓ Avoid overloading floors. Heavy furniture such as water beds, slate bedded pool tables, and heavy exercise equipment should be located over specific load bearing areas of wooden subfloors. Consult with the builder or a qualified engineer prior to placing exceptionally heavy objects on a floor to ensure the floor load capacity and deflection limits will not be exceeded.

Hardwood Floors

Comments: There are two main reasons for what may appear as discolorations in hardwood floors. First is a possible discoloration resulting from how the materials are stored and shipped. Wood floor boards that are to be sanded and finished in place are shipped in bundles. The boards in the bundle are separated by small rectangular pieces of wood called "stickers". Under moist conditions, the stickers will "bleed" into the floor boards and impart a dark color across the board. If the bleed is not severe, it can be removed when the rough floor is being sanded. Homeowners need not be concerned about this type of discoloration, as it can be corrected during installation.

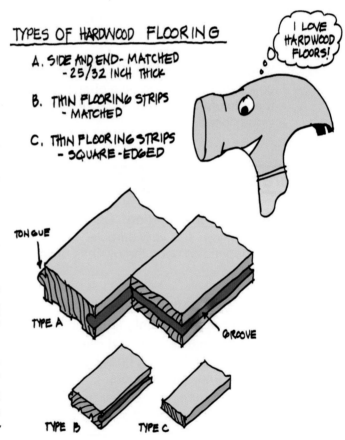

TYPES OF HARDWOOD FLOORING

A. SIDE AND END- MATCHED - 25/32 INCH THICK

B. THIN FLOORING STRIPS - MATCHED

C. THIN FLOORING STRIPS - SQUARE-EDGED

TONGUE

TYPE A

GROOVE

TYPE B   TYPE C

I LOVE HARDWOOD FLOORS!

A second possible cause of discoloration of hardwood floors can occur when pre-finished flooring is applied over a concrete slab. If moisture is trapped between the two layers, the floor boards may discolor or rot. This condition worsens when a homeowner places a rubber pad or rubber backed area rug over the floor. Although the concrete slab is likely to have a plastic *vapor barrier* under it, water vapor can pass through the slab in small amounts into the living area. The pre-finished floor boards are sealed very tightly at the factory and water vapor from the slab has difficulty passing through the wood. The addition of a rubber backed rug or tightly woven rug traps the moisture even more. While it is possible to successfully install pre-finished hardwood flooring over a concrete slab, it should be performed only by a specialty contractor who is very experienced at this trade. Homeowners should also be careful in monitoring the floor underneath any area rugs. *See Recommended Use and Maintenance below.*

Recommended Use and Maintenance:

- ✓ Examine floors carefully at the time of your walkthrough.
- ✓ Always maintain hardwood floor in accordance with the manufacturer's recommendations. Do not allow any spills or liquids to remain on floors, and do not clean floors with detergents. Use only those cleaning products recommended by the manufacturer or installer.
- ✓ Some minor random *cupping* or *crowning* can be expected over the years due to changes in humidity, and this condition is normal.
- ✓ If uniformity of color is important to you, advance arrangement should be made with the builder at the time the flooring section is completed, so that you may be present when the floor is being installed.
- ✓ Be aware that direct sunlight could can wood floors to become darker. Also, objects left on wood floors in sunny orientations can cause a permanent "shade spot".
- ✓ If a water-based liquid is spilled on the floor, or if areas of high humidity exist in poorly vented rooms, the floor boards may swell and become uneven. You should take steps to prevent this by wiping up spills quickly and using mechanical vents in laundry rooms, bathrooms and kitchens.
- ✓ If you choose to cover a pre-finished hardwood floor with an area rug, monitor the condition of the wood on a quarterly basis. You can also obtain a separate warranty from the manufacturer of the floor, or place the area rug on the concrete slab and install the wood floor around it.

Ceramic and Clay Tile Flooring

General Subject Information: Ceramic tile is a dense product with a hard surface that resists spills and scuffing. It is very durable. Clay tile is a softer material, which may be glazed or unglazed, depending upon the owner's taste. Unglazed tile requires more care because it is semi-porous.

Recommended Use and Maintenance:

- ✓ Examine floors carefully at the time of your walkthrough.
- ✓ Be aware that ceramic and clay tiles are brittle and they can be cracked, chipped or broken by placing or dropping heavy objects on them. Take care not to drop heavy objects on ceramic and clay tile floors.
- ✓ Become familiar with proper procedures for cleaning and caring for your tile floors. Grout is porous and you should seal the grout with a silicone based sealer within 30 days of occupancy.
- ✓ If acidic foods such as tomato paste or vinegar are dropped on the tile surface and allowed to remain even for a short period of time, these foods can etch and permanently stain the surface.

Granite, Marble and Other Stone Flooring

General Subject Information: Granite, marble, and other stone flooring are natural products. There are many other stone products available today such as limestone, slate and travertine. Because they are natural products, the color and veining of granite, marble, and other stone flooring are never exactly alike. Variations in appearance and installation are normal and should be expected.

Comments: Granite, marble, and other stone flooring are vulnerable to impact damage (dropping heavy items on their surfaces). Unusually heavy items (such as a grand piano or slate bedded pool table) should not be placed onto a stone floor.

Marble, granite, and tumbled stone will naturally have numerous pits and voids. Small pits are considered part of the "achieved look" of the surface and are normal and to be expected. The manufacturer or installer usually fills voids in excess of 3/8 inch in diameter. Many times what may appear to be discolorations are actually natural variations in the stone.

Recommended Use and Maintenance:
- ✔ Examine floors carefully at time of your walkthrough.
- ✔ Hairline cracks are normal and to be expected with stone flooring.
- ✔ Do not place unusually heavy items onto stone flooring, unless appropriate additional support is provided.
- ✔ Granite and marble, particularly marble, are susceptible to staining and etching by ordinary household products and fluids. Take caution with items such as vinegar, tomato paste, toilet-bowl cleaner, and cleaners containing ammonia, as they can easily stain and etch marble and granite.
- ✔ While granite and marble, particularly granite, appear to be smooth and hard, the surfaces can actually contain small pits.

Vinyl Flooring

General Subject Information: Vinyl flooring, also known as resilient flooring, is a durable, spill resistant finish floor that is very popular in kitchens, baths, and laundry rooms. Many manufacturers advertise their products as a "no wax" floor. Vinyl flooring comes in sheets and individual squares and is typically applied over a *particle board subfloor* or concrete slab.

Recommended Use and Maintenance:
- ✔ Examine floors carefully at the time of the your walkthrough
- ✔ Follow the flooring manufacturer's cleaning and care instructions for vinyl flooring.
- ✔ To extend the life of vinyl flooring, use area rugs or mats at workstations and use dirt-trapping mats at exterior doors.
- ✔ Do not allow water or other liquids to remain on vinyl flooring for long periods of time. Spills or splashes should be promptly and properly removed. Vinyl flooring is water resistant and not totally waterproof.
- ✔ Do not allow chemical or natural products with staining properties to remain on the finish floor.
- ✔ If you have vinyl flooring installed in your bathroom, inspect the caulk joint between the tub or shower pan side and the vinyl floor. Inspect every six months and recaulk when separation is visible.

Carpet Flooring

General Subject Information: Carpet is the most popular floor covering in homes. Unlike years past, today's carpets are stain resistant, wear dated, and offered in a variety of colors, fibers and weaves.

Comments: Visible seams in carpet installation are normal and to be expected, especially depending upon the type of carpet installed and the dimensions of the covered area. The visibility of seams depends on the type of carpet installed, and more importantly, on the height of the pile. Carpets with short nap, or pile, or with berber type weaves will show seams. Higher pile carpets, including plushes and shags, can be installed where seams tend not to show. Carpet is a textile product that is manufactured in 12-foot widths. If the room is wider than 12 feet, it will have a seam.

Recommended Use and Maintenance:
- ✔ Examine floors carefully at the time of your walkthrough.
- ✔ Follow the manufacturer's care and cleaning instructions.
- ✔ Do not clean carpet with improper products or allow it to remain wet for extended periods of time. Leaving carpet wet can cause mold growth in the carpet backing. Promptly clean any spills in accordance with the material manufacturer's recommendations.
- ✔ Choose carpet colors and types that will provide the longest life at sun-exposed locations. Do not let sunlight continuously beam onto carpet, as it may cause fading.
- ✔ You can expect some soiling to occur at baseboard and stair edges, even if the edges are properly sealed. This soil staining is the result of air infiltration and should be taken into consideration when selecting carpet colors. Light colors can show edge marks in a short period of time.

Plaster and Drywall

General Subject Information: Plaster and drywall are materials used to surface most of the inside walls of a house. Drywall, also known as Sheetrock®, gypsum board, or wallboard, is the predominant inside face covering. Plaster, while used exclusively 50 years ago, is used only in custom applications today. Both products have the same basic ingredients: *gypsum* and bonding or strengthening agents. While plaster is mixed and applied on the job-site, drywall is made in a factory in sheets that are typically 4 x 8 feet x ½ inch thick. Drywall is nailed or screwed to the wall studs, and the joints are covered with a paper tape and a gypsum based compound. Special corner pieces, known as *beads*, are nailed on at wall corners. When the walls are smooth, they are textured with more gypsum compound. The texturing process may be accomplished by hand troweling or by spraying with a machine. Spray texturing, which is the method of choice today, can be made with a number of different patterns such as knock down, eggshell, fog and dash. Some patterns are intentionally rough and irregular while others are supposed to be uniform throughout.

Comments: As the wood frame of the house dries, minor cracks usually appear within the first 12 months of occupancy. These cracks typically occur around door and window frames, cabinets, at the heads of windows, and where walls and ceiling planes intersect. These cracks can be easily caulked. By and large, filling, monitoring, and maintaining drywall and plaster cracks are a homeowner maintenance item. ***Refer to Recommended Use and Maintenance below***.

Surface texture is more art than science, and determining unacceptable texture is quite subjective. Hand textured walls and ceilings clearly bear the "signature" of the applicator, can be irregular, and may be nearly impossible to match by another applicator. Spray textured walls that are knocked down may have patches of texture that run together when compared to other areas. Unless these patches dominate the appearance of the wall, this is considered normal application. Areas that are not knocked down, or areas that contain numerous tool marks, are likely to be unacceptable. Texture that is fogged (light coating) and texture that is egg-shell (medium coating) is intended to have a uniform, but bumpy, appearance. The best measure of texture evaluation is consistency from wall-to-wall and from room-to-room.

Recommended Use and Maintenance:
- ✓ Minor cracks in drywall and plaster are homeowner maintenance items that may be patched with spackle or caulk.
- ✓ You should realize that wall and ceiling texturing is an art and not a precise science. Expect some irregularities. These irregularities are often more prominent at night when single light sources, such as light fixtures, cast shadows. Determining wall texture performance by feeling it is not an acceptable measure.
- ✓ Nails will sometimes back out of the drywall as the house frame dries out. This is not a structural problem, but the nails should be redriven and the heads should be spackled and painted with touchup paint.

Countertops

General Subject Information: The following types of countertop materials are commonly used in residential construction: ceramic tile, granite, marble, plastic laminate, solid surface, and cultured marble. The following comments and maintenance recommendations are for countertops in general. Refer to the specific sections that follow for a particular surface material.

Recommended Use and Maintenance:
- ✓ Examine countertops carefully at the time of your walkthrough.
- ✓ Refer to the manufacturer's recommendations for proper care and maintenance.
- ✓ Cabinets expand and shrink with room moisture. This may cause cracks between the countertop and the backsplash. Maintain these cracks with caulk or grout.

Ceramic Tile Countertops

General Subject Information: Since there are a number of different types of ceramic tile, ranging from rough handmade varieties to the very precisely manufactured types, it is impractical to apply any one standard to all ceramic tiles.

Comments: Trim tiles (the tile that caps the top or edge of a wall or countertop) are not manufactured in the same batch as the flat or field tiles. Consequently, there may be variations in color between trim and field tiles.

Recommended Use and Maintenance:

✔ Examine countertops carefully at the time of the walkthrough.

✔ Follow the manufacturer's care and cleaning recommendations for the specific ceramic tile.

✔ Re-grout or color caulk all cracks after the first year. After two years, frequent re-grouting or caulking should not be required. Tile grout should initially be sealed with a silicone based sealer the first year and then every two years.

✔ Hairline cracks may appear in grout joints where there are changes in the plane of the tile surface and where tile abuts a dissimilar material, such as at a **backsplash** or at a sink or wall. Maintain caulking and repair any incidental grout cracking, especially at backsplash and sink openings.

✔ Do not place unusually heavy objects on the tile surface, and avoid dropping things on the tiles. Tiles can loosen as a result of the improper application of **mortar**, excessive deflection of the underlying material to which tile is applied, or because of exposure to impact from heavy objects. Caulking material, colored and containing sand to match grout color, is available at local home improvement stores.

Granite, Marble, and Stone Countertops

General Subject Information: Granite, marble, and other stone countertops are natural products. There are many other stone products available today such as limestone, slate and travertine. Because they are natural products, the color and veining of granite and marble are never exactly alike. Expect variations from any installations in other similar homes. Granite, marble, and other stone surfaces are vulnerable to impact damage (dropping heavy items on their surfaces).

Recommended Use and Maintenance:

✔ Examine countertops carefully at your walkthrough.

✔ Maintain countertop in accordance with the recommendations of the material manufacturer and supplier.

✔ Maintain caulking and repair incidental grout cracking, especially at backsplash and sink openings.

✔ Do not drop heavy objects on countertops. Do not stand on countertop without a protective separation.

✔ Granite, marble, and stone can be stained by a variety of products and natural materials, such as juices.

✔ Use only cleaning products approved by the manufacturer or the applicable trade association for the material (for instance, the Marble Institute of America for granite and marble countertops).

✔ Do not use abrasives to clean any type of countertop.

✔ Avoid placing hot pots, pans, Crockpots®, etc., in direct contact with the countertop.

Plastic Laminate Countertops

General Subject Information: Plastic laminate countertops have been popular in homes for the past 50 years. They are durable and easy to maintain. These countertops are made by gluing sheets of hard plastic to a stiff **particle board** base. Small countertops can be made entirely as one piece. Larger ones, or special inlays, require seams.

<u>**Recommended Use and Maintenance:**</u>
- ✓ Examine countertops carefully at the time of your walkthrough.
- ✓ Maintain countertop in accordance with the recommendations of the material manufacturer and supplier. Maintain caulking, especially at backsplash and sink openings.
- ✓ Use only cleaning products approved by the material manufacturer; never use abrasives. Avoid placing hot objects on countertops. Plastic laminate material can scorch and melt.
- ✓ Wipe up spills immediately. Water left standing can find its way through a seam and expand the ***particle board*** backing.
- ✓ Always use a cutting board; plastic laminate can be scratched with knife blades.

Solid Surface Countertops

<u>General Subject Information:</u> "Solid surface countertops" refers to the class of plastics, called acrylic or polyester, or to a blend of plastics and fiberglass. This includes products such as Avonite™, Cerata™, Corian™, Corinthian™, Fountainhead™, Gibralter™, Hi-macs™, Staron™, Surrell™, Swanstone™, Zodiac™ and many other synthetic surfaces. Solid surface countertops are made by "fusing" (heat setting) large sections of the material to create a smooth, seamless surface. Various designs and inlays can be incorporated into the manufacturing process to create a beautiful effect.

<u>Recommended Use and Maintenance:</u>

- ✓ Do not apply countertop surface enhancers or cleansers such as Pledge™ or 409™ to a new solid surface countertop. These products will only attract and hold discoloring items such as coffee, wine or ketchup to the surface.
- ✓ Examine countertops carefully at your walkthrough.
- ✓ Maintain countertop in accordance with the recommendations of the material manufacturer and supplier.
- ✓ Do not place hot pots or dishes directly on the countertop. Use a trivet to avoid scorching and deforming. Always use a cutting board; countertops can be scratched with knives.
- ✓ Use a soft sponge or cloth with mild soap and water to clean. Remove any harsh chemicals immediately.

Cultured Marble Countertops

<u>General Subject Information:</u> A cultured marble countertop is also a synthetic countertop. Unlike the other solid surface countertops discussed in previous sections (which are considered the "new generation" of solid surface countertops), cultured marble has been around for at least 40 years. There is an upgraded version of cultured marble known as "onyx". Onyx has a smoother top and more uniform color spread than basic cultured marble. Cultured marble also has an application for bathtub and shower surrounds.

Color swirls can vary significantly in cultured marble due to the fact that each batch is made like a marble cake. In general, the color swirls should be consistent throughout the top, and should not be concentrated in any one spot.

<u>**Recommended Use and Maintenance:**</u>
- ✓ Examine countertops carefully at your walkthrough.
- ✓ Maintain countertop in accordance with the recommendations of the material manufacturer and supplier.
- ✓ Do not drop heavy objects on countertop surfaces.
- ✓ Cigarettes, curling irons, and other hot objects will burn and discolor cultured marble.
- ✓ Never cut directly on cultured marble as sharp objects will scratch the surface.

Appliances

<u>**General Subject Information:**</u> In a house there are two broad categories of appliances: (1) kitchen type appliances such as the dishwasher, oven and range and (2) system appliances, such as the furnace, air conditioner, water heater, and gas burning fireplace. Smoke detectors are also considered appliances.

<u>**Recommended Use and Maintenance:**</u>
- ✓ If a registration card is provided, register all appliances with the manufacturer.
- ✓ Read and follow the manufacturer's operating instructions.
- ✓ Before making a service call, follow the Trouble Shooting Guide found at the back of most appliance owners' manuals.
- ✓ If an appliance trips a *breaker*, most likely the circuit is overloaded or the appliance is defective. If the appliance is portable, try using a circuit in another room. If the appliance works in the other room, the original circuit was probably overloaded. Do not continue to use an appliance that repeatedly trips a breaker.

Cabinets and Vanities

<u>**General Subject Information:**</u> Cabinets and vanities are an attractive addition to beautify and provide functional storage in kitchens, baths, and laundries. Wood, either painted or stained, is the most popular choice followed by plastic laminate and faux wood vinyl.

There are common use and care procedures for cabinets and vanities; all of which can be achieved by proper homeowner use and maintenance. ***Refer to Recommended Use and Maintenance below***:

(1) Prevent the finish from wearing prematurely. Cabinet finishes tend to age more in hot, humid rooms and in areas that surround sinks due to water that is splashed on the finish. Cabinets in contact with water and lack of proper maintenance are major contributing factors to warping. Over time and without proper care, plastic laminate cabinets can delaminate at joints and corners. This usually occurs as a result of water getting into the core of the cabinet door.

(2) Prevent the drawer slide brackets from failing. Drawer guides that support the drawer opening commonly fail. They are often made of plastic and may break over time. This is a very inexpensive replacement item that can be purchased at a hardware store. Drawers should not be overloaded, and should be operated in a smooth fashion. Both doors and drawers should be operated without slamming the drawers shut.

(3) Keep cabinets and cabinet doors flush and aligning. Gaps appear between cabinet cases or doors that do not align. As the house acclimates to the rough framing materials, the structure will have a tendency to contract when the rough lumber dries out. This has the potential to affect interior finishes and is considered normal. Hinges can also become loose and occasionally may need to be retightened or adjusted.

Recommended Use and Maintenance:

- ✓ Use caution when loading upper cabinets so as to not overload them. Heavy plates and dishes and canned goods do not belong in upper cabinets. Refer to "**Ten Most Common Mistakes Made By Homeowners**" in the Introduction.

- ✓ Maintain all cabinets, particularly any cabinetry that is located in areas that are subject to moisture, such as kitchens, bathrooms or laundry rooms. Water should not be allowed to remain on any wood products, whether sealed or not. Maintenance consists of keeping surfaces dry and clean, polishing wood surfaces, and keeping hinges lubricated.

- ✓ Be careful not to overload the drawers. This puts additional stress on the guides causing them to prematurely fail.

- ✓ Operate doors and drawers smoothly and easily. Metal drawer guides should be lubricated with light lubricating oil every two years.

- ✓ Doors can go out of adjustment, depending upon their care and use. Do not slam, hang objects from, or pull on the door, as this will cause hinge mechanisms to weaken not only at their fastening points but also within the mechanisms themselves. Periodically inspect hinges and retighten if necessary.

- ✓ Liquids should be cleaned up immediately and not left on a surface, particularly at joints or corners. This creates the potential for breakdown of the glues used to laminate the surface to the substrate.

- ✓ If you have painted wood cabinets, you can expect, over time, for a gap to appear at the vertical joint where the two cabinet sections are joined together.

- ✓ If an uneven or larger gap appears where two cabinet doors close together, this gap can be narrowed or straightened by turning the adjustment screw on the hinge with a screwdriver.

Finishes

Comments: Cabinet finishes are created two ways: (1) as a completely finished module that is painted, laminated or stained in a factory, or (2) as a larger component that is made in a cabinet shop and painted or stained after it is installed in the house. Cabinets that are stained to show the **grain** of the wood will have irregularities in the finish color. This is due to the fact that no two pieces of wood have exactly the same characteristics. Stain absorbs differently through flat surfaces, soft grains, and ends. Painted cabinets should be reasonably uniform in color because there is no intention to show the grain. Painted cabinets may be made of materials other than wood. As long as the same paint or stain is used for the entirety of the cabinets, slight irregularities in the appearance of the stain or paint are considered normal.

Recommended Use and Maintenance:

- ✓ Be aware that painted cabinets will separate somewhat at the **stiles** (vertical joints) due to normal drying out of the house frame.
- ✓ Bathroom and laundry fans should always be operating when those rooms are in use.
- ✓ Never allow water to remain on the cabinet surface, as this will cause damage to the finish.

✓ Cabinets, drawer fronts and doors need to be periodically inspected for excessive wear or deterioration of the finish.

✓ Consider stained cabinets as furniture and treat the wood faces with furniture polish.

Moldings and Trim

General Subject Information: Interior trim, also called finish trim, is divided into two categories: standing trim and running trim. Standing trim is used for window and door casings. Running trim is used for baseboards, crown or chair molding.

Comments: Minor separation at the joints may occur as a result of expansion and contraction of the house. This occurs as the lumber in the house starts to dry out and stabilize. Expansion and contraction may also occur during seasonal changes in humidity. Minor separations may also occur where molding abuts one another or abuts another material. Wood has an inherent characteristic of hairline cracking, which is an unavoidable condition and small cracks should be maintained and filled by homeowners.

Recommended Use and Maintenance:

✓ Examine moldings and trim carefully at the time of the walkthrough, and be sure to check for any splitting or checking of the wood.

✓ Gaps in trim and molding resulting from the settling of the house frame are routine maintenance items. If the gaps are minor, putty or caulk, sand and then refinish in order to prevent any further splitting or separation to the molding or trim.

✓ Depending on the climate and environment where the house is located, wood products like moldings and trim may need more than normal maintenance. If cracks occur, it is vital to seal them by caulking or puttying, followed by sanding and refinishing. This prevents moisture from migrating to the unprotected back side of the wood which can cause twisting and warping.

Mirrors

General Subject Information: A mirror is a combination of high quality glass and a thin layer of silver or aluminum applied to the back side. The glass supports the metallic layer and will protect its shiny surface. Silvering quality glass is specially selected glass, which is exceptionally free of imperfections and other irregularities and is used in mirror and optical applications. A second grade is mirror glazing, which is also a superior glass for mirrors. Both silvering glass and mirror quality glass have very low distortion levels and must be smooth to within 1/25,000 inch.

FILL GAP

SPACKLE

APPLY SPACKLE TO INTERIOR TRIM. THEN, PAINT OVER THE SPACKLE

Comments: A scratch, or scratches, do not constitute a safety concern, but tends to be more of a visual distraction. Cracked glass may present a safety issue and should be replaced by a professional glazing company as soon as possible.

Recommended Use and Maintenance:

✓ Inspect all mirrors at the time of your walkthrough for any irregularities within the glazing and its metallic backing.

✓ When cleaning a mirror, use caution when using cleansers that contain ammonia or vinegar. Ammonia and vinegar are excellent glass cleaners, however they can be extremely damaging to the metallic backing of the mirror.

✓ Do not apply cleansers over the top or sides of mirrors, and do not allow cleansers to get into the track at the bottom of the mirror. Manufacturers often recommend applying cleaning agents to a cloth, and then wiping down the mirror.

Shower and Tub Enclosures

General Subject Information: Tub and shower enclosures have replaced the traditional shower rod and curtain. They are designed to keep water contained within the tub and shower surrounds. This is a high maintenance area within the house and one deserving of close use and maintenance attention.

Comments: Keeping shower and tub enclosures watertight is a duty of the homeowner. Except under unusual cases where the plastic or rubber parts used to keep water inside the tub or shower are missing, leaks at the door or sliding panel are due to two causes: (1) the bather has directed the shower head at the joint between the door and the fixed panel, or (2) the sliding panels at the tub have had their direction reversed by the bather. The inside panel must be the one closest to the shower head for proper use.

Fiberglass and acrylic tubs and showers will have a certain degree of flex depending upon how the unit was manufactured and the weight of the occupant. Some flexing is to be expected and each manufacturer furnishes installation instructions regarding their products.

Recommended Use and Maintenance:

✓ Inspect the shower and tub enclosures carefully at the time of the walkthrough for any scratches in the glass or plastic.

✓ Seal the tile grout prior to use, with a silicone-based sealer that can be purchased at any hardware store. Seal annually thereafter.

✓ Become aware of the proper use of a tub and shower enclosure. Keep shower water directed away from the door and panels.

✓ Continuous leaking may result in rot of the **underlayment** and **subfloor**. Continuous leaking also creates an environment for mold and mildew growth and for termites.

✓ Clean out weep holes regularly.

KEEP CLEAN

USE A JUMBO PAPER CLIP TO CLEAN SHOWER DOOR TRACK WEEP HOLES

✓ Caulk joints in bathrooms need to be inspected and re-caulked every six months. This includes the joint at the bottom, of the shower, the joint between the tub and the wall, the joint where the tub or shower pan meets the floor, and vertical inside corners and seats. It is very important that these joints do not pass any water. Unseen dryrot and mold can accumulate for years.

✓ Any mold or mildew found in bathrooms should be removed as soon as possible with a strong mildewcide. The cause of the mold or mildew should be found (example: a leaky window or the failure to use bathroom fan) and eliminated.

✓ Caulking of the enclosure on a regular basis is an important maintenance item. Be sure to remove all of the old caulk before applying the new caulk.

✓ The first row of tile around the shower floor or the top of the tub is susceptible to cracking and should be inspected and cracks filled accordingly.

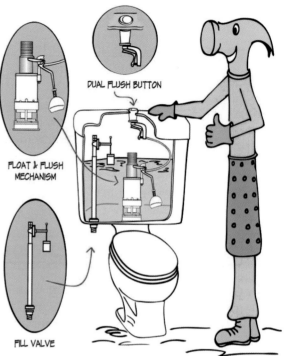

DUAL FLUSH TOILETS HELP SAVE WATER

DUAL FLUSH BUTTON

FLOAT & FLUSH MECHANISM

FILL VALVE

✓ When significant cracking first appears, the grout joints should be caulked with a caulking compound made for bathroom use. Many grout manufacturers also make flexible sealants to match their grouts.

Green Tip! Prevent leaks. One leaking toilet can waste 1,000 gallons of water in one month.

Drywall

Comments: Your tub and shower surround may not extend to the ceiling. If it does not, the area between the surround and the ceiling is likely to be drywall that has been textured and painted. Because water splashes on tub and tile surround surfaces (even though they may be covered in tile or some other hard water resistant finish), water and water vapor can penetrate the surface. Over time, water penetration may cause underlying wood or ordinary drywall to fail. Avoiding this is an essential homeowner maintenance item.

Recommended Use and Maintenance:
✓ Make certain that a coat of premium enamel paint is maintained on the drywall surface.
✓ Maintain the caulking between the tub or shower pan and the first row of tile (**see Homeowner Maintenance Summary**).
✓ Do not allow water to remain on bathroom surfaces. Wipe dry after each use.
✓ Always use the mechanical fan, or open a window to help reduce condensation and moisture.

Paint and Stain

For interior paint and stain maintenance recommendations, refer to *Chapter 5, "Paint and Stain"*.

Chapter Seven

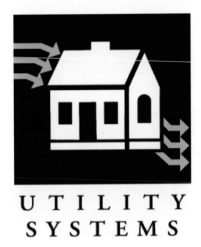

U T I L I T Y
S Y S T E M S

includes:

Heating:
Forced Air
Radiant

Cooling:
Air Conditioning
Evaporative Cooling

Electrical

Plumbing:
Piping
Faucets
Sinks
Tubs/Showers
Toilets
Water Heaters

Fire Sprinkler System

Telephone

Cable TV

Utility Systems

Heating

General Subject Information: While there are several systems available to heat a house, including combustion, electric and solar, the focus of this chapter will be on the two most common systems: <u>forced air systems</u> and <u>radiant heat systems</u>.

Forced Air Systems

Forced air systems consist of a combustion or electric furnace, plus a series of large pipes in the attic and crawl space known as ducts. Ducts supply warm air to the ceiling, floor, or walls of the house. The forced air system also has a return air component that circulates the air back to the heat source. Some forced air furnaces may use natural gas, bottled gas, fuel oil, wood pellets, or coal as a source of heat. Natural gas is the most common fuel in most areas of the United States. Less frequently used systems are heat pumps and electric furnaces. Electric furnaces operate solely with electricity. Heat pumps are reverse air conditioners that also operate on electricity. Heat pumps take heat from the air outside a house and transfer it to inside the house. Even on very cold days there is a small amount of heat present in the outside air. In the summertime, the heat pump operates like a standard air conditioner. Heat pumps are typically installed in geographic regions where natural gas is not available.

Radiant Heat Systems

Radiant heat systems use either tubing filled with warm fluid or electrical wires that are heated to transmit radiant energy into the living space of the house. The system that uses tubing circulates a warm fluid, usually water or a light oil, through the tubes, which may be located along the baseboard or embedded in a concrete floor. Like the forced air system, the heat source to heat the fluid comes from burning natural gas or fuel oil. The flame heats the fluid in a small boiler and a pump circulates the hot fluid throughout the tubing in the house.

The radiant heat system using oil or water to transfer heat from the boiler to the slab is known as a closed loop system. Fluid is heated in the boiler and pumped to the floor or baseboard. There, it gives off its heat, and then the cooler fluid is returned to the boiler to be reheated.

Radiant systems using electricity rely upon electrical resistance (much like the wires inside an ordinary household toaster) to create heat. The electrical heat strips are found either in the floor or ceilings of houses. While the electrical resistance system has a low cost to install, it is rarely used anymore because it has a high cost to operate.

Radiant systems provide a quiet operation of uniform warmth, but they do not circulate air through the house as a forced air system does. A device called a thermostat controls the temperature of both types of systems. There is at least one thermostat in the house, perhaps more depending upon how many zones are created for heating within the house.

Many factors control interior comfort for heating a house. Some factors include:
- → the orientation of rooms in the house
- → the amount of window area in a room
- → whether the windows are shaded with a drapery that could provide additional insulation
- → the amount of insulation installed
- → the type of windows and exterior doors installed
- → the ceiling height or "volume" of the rooms

Comments: Many factors affect the performance of heating systems. The most important is system design. Other factors include placement of furniture, solar orientation of the room, and location of the room in the house. For example, a room located above a thermostat will be warmer in winter than a room located below the thermostat. The downstairs room will be cooler in both summer and winter; this is because warm air rises to the ceiling and cool air falls to the floor.

The *air handler* fan (blower) will make noise as it blows warm air throughout the house. Noise will also be heard as air flows back to the furnace through the return air system. The architectural design of the house often puts restrictions on the design of the heating system. As a result, the system may have a noise level that is irritating to some occupants.

Occasionally, there may be a booming noise created when the heating system is first turned on or when cooling down. This condition that sometimes occurs in forced air heating systems is known as the "oil canning" effect. The noise is a result of a large area of sheet metal being rapidly heated or cooled. Be aware that the resulting noise may not be able to be mitigated.

Another type of booming noise in forced air heating systems is caused by the delay created when the furnace burner ignites too late. A larger volume of gas accumulates and is not ignited (burned) soon enough, creating a small explosive effect in the furnace. If you hear a booming noise when the furnace is turned on, notify the builder immediately.

Recommended Use and Maintenance:

- ✓ Be aware that it is not possible to achieve a uniform temperature throughout the house. A difference in temperature will exist between the thermostat location and other rooms, particularly if those rooms are located above or below the thermostat location.
- ✓ Large window areas should be properly draped or otherwise protected from heat loss, and no furniture or other devices should be placed in rooms so as to impede the airflow. Most air supply grills (registers) have dampers that can be adjusted in rooms for the difference in the summer and winter temperature needs.
- ✓ Change or clean the furnace filter according to the manufacturer's recommendations (usually no less than every six months). A dirty filter reduces airflow and causes the system to use more energy.

FIRST, YOU DETERMINE WHETHER THE FILTER IS IN THE ATTIC OR THE CLOSET... -THEN, REPLACE IT WITH THE SAME SIZE

✓ Check the thermostat periodically and, if applicable, change the batteries when it is indicated that batteries are weak. Do not leave dead batteries in a thermostat, especially during months when the system is not being used. Dead batteries can leak and corrode the thermostat.

✓ If a booming noise is heard when the furnace is turned on, notify the builder.

✓ If your home is heated with a radiant system, it usually requires very little maintenance. However, if make-up fluid constantly needs to be added to the system, there may be a leak. Leaks should be reported immediately since they can cause the soil to swell and undermine the slab.

✓ Be aware that aftermarket contractors who install alarm systems or pest control companies have well-deserved reputations for tearing and squashing ductwork in attics and crawl spaces. If you are having work done of this nature, inspect the crawl space or attic both prior to and after the work is done, to ensure that all ductwork remains intact.

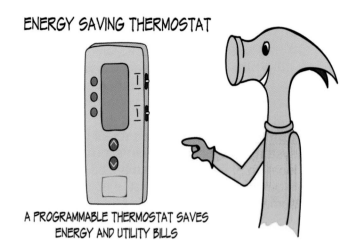

ENERGY SAVING THERMOSTAT

A PROGRAMMABLE THERMOSTAT SAVES ENERGY AND UTILITY BILLS

ENERGY STAR® APPLIANCES SAVE SIGNIFICANT ENERGY

Handy's Hint:

All vents, including kitchen hood filters, bathroom laundry fans and dryer vents, should be removed and cleaned. The kitchen hood filters should be washed about four times a year. Dryer vent ducts should be cleaned every two to five years.

WHOLE HOUSE VENTILATION FAN - RUNS 24/7

A. TURN OFF BREAKER AND THEN GENTLY PULL DOWN COVER WITH YOUR FINGER TIPS

B. WASH COVER WITH MILD SOAP AND WARM WATER

C. VACUUM INSIDE OF FAN

Cooling

General Subject Information: Regional climates vary significantly from communities near an ocean which have little or no need for central air conditioning, to communities in the inland or plains regions which may experience many summer days in excess of 100 degrees F. Typically, central air conditioning systems are installed as part of the indoor comfort package of the house. Most central air conditioning systems share the same *air handler*, duct work, and return air systems as the heating system. Homes that are built with air conditioning or "prepped" for future air conditioning will have larger ducts than homes that are built for heating only. Therefore, homeowners should not assume that air conditioning can be installed successfully at a later date, if the home was built as heat-only. The difference between a house that has central air conditioning and one that does not is the addition of a circular or box-like unit called the condenser that is outside the house (or sometimes on the roof). A cooling coil is also added inside the furnace. Almost all central air conditioning systems use electricity as their power source.

Another type of cooling system used less frequently in residential construction is the evaporative cooler, commonly known as the "swamp cooler". Like central air conditioning systems, evaporative coolers use some of the same components of the heating system such as the ductwork. The evaporative cooler is usually mounted on the roof, and the cooling effect is a result of air being drawn through wetted filter pads. While evaporative coolers are cheaper to operate than central air conditioning, they are less efficient in their cooling operation and may increase the humidity levels within the home.

Homes that are heated with radiant heating typically do not have central air conditioning, as there is no ductwork system to deliver cool air into the rooms. Central air conditioning can be installed in homes with radiant heating using ductwork, air handlers and condensers, but the system is totally separate from the heating system.

Comments: Air conditioning systems are typically installed as part of a package that must often qualify under a state or federal energy conservation requirements. Factors such as the solar orientation of the house (facing south and west), and the amount of glass area within a room can influence the effectiveness of air conditioning. Rooms with windows facing west and south should have window coverings that are capable of reducing 50% of the heat gain to the room.

In a typical central air conditioning system, the *condensate line* is typically a white plastic or copper pipe that comes out of the air handler portion of the furnace and discharges through an outside wall. Because the water is cool and the discharge is slow, the condensate line provides an attractive environment for algae to grow. Systems are installed with a primary line and secondary condensate lines. The primary line goes through a trap and then discharges near the outside

foundation (or in some locations into a sewer trap). The secondary condensate line discharges above a window or patio door (if the air conditioner coil is in the attic furnace) or in the garage or other prominent place (if the air conditioner is located in the furnace in that area). The reason why the secondary condensate line is located in a prominent location is that it should only discharge when the primary line is plugged and you should be able to see this condition. *Refer to Recommended Use and Maintenance below*.

Most air conditioning systems have a redundant safety feature consisting of a circuit breaker in the main panel and a fuse box near the condenser. Homeowners often encounter a situation where a functioning air conditioning system shut off in the fall will not start when it comes time to turn it on in the spring. Typically, this condition can be traced to one or two blown fuses or tripped circuit breakers. When the compressor remains idle during the winter months, its internal parts become resistant to turning. This resistance often results in a blown fuse or tripped circuit breaker when first turned on in springtime.

Recommended Use and Maintenance:

✓ In rooms that have the potential for high heat gain, such as sun porches, solariums, and other rooms with a large number of skylights and windows, you should consider installation of solar blocking devices. Sunshades are typical.

✓ Prevent children from playing around air conditioning condensers. Fingers and fan blades are not compatible.

✓ Maintain the manufacturer's recommended clearance between the condenser and any landscaping, fencing, or other structures.

✓ Condensate lines should be inspected twice a year: at the beginning of the air conditioning season and at the end. If a trickle discharge is reduced to an occasional drip, it could mean that the condensate line is in the process of becoming plugged. Another symptom of a plugged condensate line is cold water droplets blowing out of the air supply grills in the house. If water is observed dripping in front of a window or patio door, or onto a garage floor, it is likely that the primary condensate line is plugged. If this occurs, shut off the air conditioner and schedule the system for servicing.

✓ Once every two months, on warm winter days, the air conditioner should be started and run for a few minutes to keep the internal parts clean and lubricated. This will prevent blown fuses or tripped breakers and keep the internal parts in smooth operating condition.

✓ Evaporative coolers need to be kept clean and free of mineral build-up in order to operate properly. Depending upon local water quality, evaporative coolers need to be treated and backwashed periodically.

✓ **CAUTION**: Do not tint the inside pane of dual pane glass; it may cause the seals to fail. Refer to ***Ten Most Common Mistakes Made by Homeowners*** in the Introduction.

✓ Furnace filters need to be changed in the summer, too. Warm summer air contains more dust than wet winter air.

Electrical

General Subject Information: The electrical system in homes is installed in compliance with the National Electric Code (NEC). Most cities and counties in the United States have adopted this Code. Among other things, the NEC deals with wire size, circuits, breakers, and placement of outlets.

Comments: Flickering lights can indicate a possible overload or poor connection somewhere in the branch circuit. If a heavy-duty motor driven appliance is plugged into a wall outlet, it is likely to cause momentary flickering of the lights when it is first turned on. High capacity appliances should not be plugged into standard wall outlets.

Fuses and circuit breakers are electricity's safety valves. When a fuse blows, it must be replaced. When a circuit breaker trips, it can be reset. Most houses today are equipped with circuit breakers in the main panel (outside) or in the *subpanel* (inside). Special appliances like furnaces and air conditioning condensers have their own fuse boxes or circuit breakers. Usually when frequent tripping occurs, it is a sign that the circuit is being overused. As circuit breakers get older, they tend to wear out and trip more easily.

A *ground fault interrupter (GFI)*, sometimes designated as a GFCI circuit, is an especially sensitive breaker that is located in or tied to the outlets in the kitchen, baths, outdoors, and the garage. Appliances manufactured outside of the United States, (although they may carry a *UL label*) are notorious for tripping GFIs. When a GFI trips it can be reset at the outlet that has the small black button or inside the subpanel. **Refer to the illustration below.**

While most household small wiring is copper, the larger wires (known as cables) typically are aluminum. All wires are covered with insulation. Aluminum cables are often used to provide power to air conditioners, heat pumps and electric ovens. Aluminum is a softer metal than copper and over times, it can deform or "creep" where it is connected. When aluminum creep occurs, the connection is no longer tight and sparking jumps through the gap. Appliances will consume more power and breakers will trip.

Light fixtures, especially ones with a bright brass finish, will tarnish. The rate of tarnish depends upon outdoor and indoor air pollution and the degree to which the finish was coated with a protective film. It is very important not to use a higher wattage bulb in a light fixture than the wattage recommended by the manufacturer.

If a bedroom does not have a ceiling light, at least one wall outlet (one plug only, not both) to a wall will be connected to the switch near the door. Unless the switch is on, any light or appliance plugged into the outlet will not operate. This is often mistaken for a non-performing outlet.

Amounts of noise from exhaust fans vary by manufacturer. Exhaust fans are required to exchange a certain volume of air in the room per hour. As long as the plastic or metal fan blades are turning freely, they are likely to be operating as intended. If the fan blades are hitting something solid, like the fan housing, they will make a distinct battering noise.

Recommended Use and Maintenance:

- ✓ Avoid overloading circuits with multiple appliances and add-on outlets.
- ✓ If wires feel warm to the touch, they should be unplugged and reinserted into a separate circuit.
- ✓ Note: Circuit breakers are found in the main panel where the meter is located or in the *subpanel* (the gray metal panel typically located in the hallway, laundry room or bedroom of the house). The circuits are labeled inside the panels.
- ✓ DO NOT replace a fuse or circuit breaker with one that has a higher rating or one made by a different manufacturer! This action could result in a fire.
- ✓ GFCIs and Arc Interrupters should be tested monthly. Pressing the **TEST** button should cause the RESET button to pop out. Push in the RESET to restore the circuit. If the GFCI will not reset, it may be faulty or there may be an open circuit. Contact a licensed electrical contractor to check the circuit.

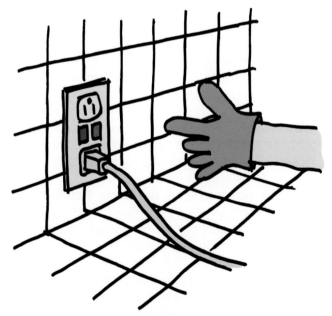

TEST G.F.I. OUTLETS MONTHLY
- IT'S EASY TO DO:
"TEST" IS BLACK; "RESET" IS RED

✔ Do not plug a freezer or refrigerator into a GFI outlet.

✔ If there is a current surge or power failure, a tripped GFI will not reset itself. Your freezer or garage refrigerator may be off and you would not know it until the food spoils. Be sure to not overload circuits to the point where fuses blow or breakers trip. If frequent tripping occurs, you should notify the builder.

✔ Inspect fixtures during the walkthrough. Check with fixture manufacturers regarding their warranty. Fixtures, especially bright brass, will need to be cleaned and polished as routine maintenance.

✔ Do not disconnect the bath or laundry fans because they create an annoying noise. Moist air must be exhausted to the outside; otherwise mold and mildew can form on the walls and ceiling. Fans should be operated while these rooms are in use.

✔ Light bulbs in the closet must be **covered with a lens or globe as part of the fixture. When changing** bulbs in the closet, make sure you do not exceed the manufacturer's recommended wattage for the bulb requirement and do not leave the fixture cover off. Lights left on in closets, especially with halogen bulbs, can generate a significant amount of heat and poses a fire hazard.

✔ If aluminum wiring is used in the house, it is recommended that the terminal connections of aluminum cables be inspected and tightened if necessary by a qualified, licensed electrical contractor within the first two years after occupancy.

Plumbing

General Subject Information: The plumbing system in a house consists of three main components: water supply piping, wastewater piping, and fixtures. Gas piping is a separate system used to convey natural or LP gas to appliances such as furnaces, water heaters, stoves, cook tops, ovens, fireplaces, and barbeques.

Both copper and plastic are used for water supply piping in homes, but historically copper has been the most prominent material used. Waste piping, which carries wastewater from the fixtures in the house, is typically black plastic piping called **ABS**. Alternatively, some municipalities require waste piping to be copper or cast iron, or a combination of both. Unless the house is connected to a septic tank, wastewater flows in a sewer to a local sewage treatment plant.

Wastewater piping also has pipes that protrude through the roof of the house called vents. The purpose of the vents is to allow the wastewater to flow through the pipes without becoming "air locked". The vents also help to dissipate odors.

"Fixtures" refers to items like toilets, bathtubs, and sinks. Nearly all plumbing fixtures have *traps*, which prevent sewer gases from backing into the house. Traps can be seen under the sink and are the U-shaped part of the piping where wastewater sits and blocks the flow of sewer gases. Toilets have traps built into the bowls.

Some water suppliers do not recommend the installation of water softeners as they may make the water more corrosive and lead to early pipe deterioration. Check with your water supplier prior to any water softener installation.

Depending upon local regulations, the house may be fitted with a fire sprinkler system. The system consists of water under pressure in pipes that, in the event of fire, will spray water through the sprinkler heads located in the ceilings and walls. Unless there is a fire or excessive source of heat, the fire sprinkler system remains passive. However, routine testing of the fire sprinkler system is very important.

Comments: Many plumbing problems occur because of freezing weather. In geographic areas where freezing weather is common and part of the normal weather pattern, unprotected pipes may leak at valves and joints during subfreezing temperatures. Some safeguards include: bringing the water supply line into the interior of the house (not an outside wall); using deep seat valves on hose bibs; wrapping pipes in unheated areas with thermostatic controlled heat tape; and providing a drain down valve at the lowest accessible part of the water supply system. Refer to the "*Winterizing Your Home*" section in the Introduction.

Backed up drainage systems, particularly toilets, can also be a common problem. For the vast majority of incidents, the homeowners have caused this condition. A federal law requires that all toilets installed in new construction flush with 1.6 gallons of water or less. Homeowners who are used to larger capacity toilets (3.5 or 7 gallon flush) sometimes have difficulty making the transition to low flush toilets. It is very important that each toilet is flushed and the water is turned on to each fixture during the **walkthrough** process. Homeowners should also take care to learn the proper use of all their fixtures. *Refer to Recommended Use and Maintenance below*.

Water pressure problems arise from two sources: (1) inadequate pressure from the water supply agency in their piping system, or (2) the piping system in the house is undersized. Most plumbing systems are designed to operate within the range of 15 psi (pounds per square inch) and 80 psi, measured at the point where the water supply pipe enters the house. High water pressure can be a problem because it creates a condition known as "***water hammer***" and causes noise and banging of the pipes. High water pressure can be reduced with a special pressure-reducing valve. Low water pressure can be increased with the use of a booster pump. It should be noted that all showerheads and most sink faucets are required to have flow restrictors placed in them for water conservation. Reduced flows from flow restrictors may give a mistaken impression of low water pressure.

WATER HEATERS
SHOULD BE SECURELY
STRAPPED TO THE
HOUSE FRAME TO
AVOID TIP-OVER

In most houses, the source of hot water is a water heater. The source of heat for the water heater is likely to be natural gas or LP gas. In areas where gas is not available, electric water heaters are permitted. There are several factors that could contribute to a lack of hot water: a power failure that cuts off the supply of gas or electricity; the pilot light has gone out; a malfunctioning water heater; a temperature setting too low on the water heater, or heat loss through the piping system, particularly at far ends of the house. Typically the water heater installer will set the water temperature between a low of 120 degrees F and a high of 140 degrees F. Before changing the temperature on your water heater, refer to ***Recommended Use and Maintenance below***.

In geographic areas where humidity is high, condensation may form on the outside of cold water lines, gas lines and toilet tanks. Cold water inside the pipe creates a cooling effect. Resulting condensation on the outside of water lines is normal and can be expected.

Faucets are manufactured with either a washer or cartridge to prevent leakage when the faucet is turned off. Cartridges have 10 times or greater the useful life of washers. The quality of the water supply affects the useful life of both cartridges and washers. Both municipal water and well water contain a certain amount of very small particles of solid material. Over time, this may affect the performance of washers and cartridges. ***Refer to Recommended Use and Maintenance below.***

Sink and tub stoppers are not designed to create a perfect seal. A perfect seal is not necessary for customary and usual use. Sink and tub stoppers easily get out of adjustment through continuous use and can be affected by debris trapped in the drain.

As concrete is certain to crack, brass bathroom fittings are certain to tarnish. Most brass fittings are coated with lacquer. Eventually the lacquer chips or is rubbed off, and the brass tarnishes. The degree of tarnish depends upon the amount of use, the water quality, and pollutants present in the air. Some manufacturers offer a lifetime finish on their brass fittings.

The connection between the pipe and the floor and the toilet base is made with a wax ring. This wax has the same inside diameter as the pipe flange. A portion of the wax ring fits slightly into the pipe. Pressing the toilet onto the wax ring makes a complete seal. When a toilet leaks at the floor, the chances are that the seal of the wax ring has failed. Wax rings dry out and become brittle over a period of time.

Recommended Use and Maintenance:

- ✓ In the event of detecting the odor of leaking gas, shut off the gas supply to the fixture. If the location of the gas leak cannot be easily determined, shut off the gas at the meter, evacuate the house, and call the gas company from a neighbor's house or from a phone outside of the house.
- ✓ Notify the builder if you notice any gas or liquid leaks in piping, no matter how small. Failure to give timely notice can result in health hazards, personal injury, and structural damage.
- ✓ To protect against the nuisance of infrequent freezing (extreme) weather, you may want to purchase protective materials such as pipe insulation and electric resistant heat tape (usually sold at local hardware stores). If the house is going to be unoccupied for a period of time during possible freezing weather, the thermostat should be set on "Heat" at its minimum setting.
- ✓ Sink, tub, and shower traps should be kept free and clear as routine maintenance items. Material such as hair or toothpaste may accumulate in the traps and could eventually cause a back up. Try to keep these materials from getting into the trap in the first place, and use a drain cleaner every 60 days to keep the traps scoured out and free from debris build-up.
- ✓ In areas where the water service is at the lower end of the allowable pressure range, water flows from fixtures will be less. This should be addressed with the agency that supplies the water. If the problem persists, consider installing a booster pump to increase pressure. Using several fixtures simultaneously may also result in low water flow and decrease in pressure.
- ✓ Sewer gas smells coming from drains typically indicate a lack of water in the trap. This occurs when a drain is not used for long periods of time and the water evaporates from the trap. Pouring a large glass of water in the drain will fill the trap sufficiently.
- ✓ Washers and cartridges should be replaced at the time when dripping is first noticed. Many cartridges have a 5-year to lifetime guarantee on parts. Most of the current bathroom and kitchen faucets are made with cartridges which require only infrequent replacement. Hose bibs (the valves that a hose is connected to on the outside of the house) are made with washers. Depending upon the amount of use, hose bib washers may need to be replaced as frequently as every six months or as infrequently as every 3 years. If leaking occurs at the "stem" or handle of the valve (often at the hose bib or water heater), the nut at the base of the stem can be tightened or repacked to solve this problem.

✔ Toilet tanks contain mechanical parts inside that wear out over time. Depending upon the amount of use and water quality, replacing worn flappers, floats, and valves may be necessary as once a year or as infrequently as every 10 years. Water supplies with a high mineral concentration (known as **hard water**) will leave deposits inside the toilet tank and its parts. This condition will cause more frequent replacement and rebuilding of toilet parts than areas without a high mineral content in the water supply.

✔ Frequent demand over short time periods (such as morning showers by an entire family) can result in a lack of hot water until the water heater has had time to recover. If you wish to increase water temperature, do so by adjusting the control dial on most water heaters. Electric water heaters are often pre-set and cannot be adjusted. It is very important to recognize that the higher the temperature setting, the greater the danger of scalding. **CAUTION!** Before entering the tub or shower, always turn on water and adjust it to a safe and proper temperature. Children, the elderly, or any disabled persons should never be placed in a tub or shower before the water is turned on and the temperature safely adjusted.

✔ Notify the builder of leaking toilets before additional damage occurs. Toilets that leak will cause structural damage if the toilet is located over a wood subfloor. A toilet that leaks creates a condition for termites to enter the house, regardless of whether it sits on a wooden subfloor or a concrete slab. Termites are attracted to dark, damp conditions in the soil. It is important to note that a toilet that rocks back and forth or moves side-to-side may be leaking, even though no leak is visible.

✔ DO NOT put drain cleaner into a garbage disposal. It may corrode the cutting blade edges. Every four or five years, sink traps will need to be removed and cleaned.

✔ Monthly cleaning and maintenance of mechanical sink and tub stoppers is a routine maintenance item.

✔ Brass is a beautiful but "soft" metal. It is easily scratched and tarnished. Follow the manufacturer's instructions when cleaning brass. Cleansers with abrasives and cleansers with ammonia are likely to scratch and chemically attack brass finishes.

✔ To prolong the life of a tank-type water heater, accumulated sediment should be removed from the heater tank once a year. This task can be performed by attaching a thick wall garden hose to the drain spigot at the bottom of the tank and draining out <u>no more</u> than two gallons. Since the water being drained is very hot, be careful that the hot water does not come into contact with persons, animals, plants or any material that could be damaged by scalding water.

✔ Although many gas water heaters today have automatic ignition systems, you should become familiar with how to manually light a water heater pilot because you may be faced with an automatic ignition failure.

✔ As electric water heaters age, the heating element can wear out and fall to the bottom of the tank. If this condition occurs, the circuit breaker cannot be reset and the water heater should be replaced.

Fire Sprinkler System

General Subject Information: Many jurisdictions in the country require automatic fire sprinklers to be installed in homes, particularly in condominiums and townhouses. Periodic testing of the system and alarms must be done, subject to local regulations.

Recommended Use and Maintenance:
- ✓ Do not paint any fire sprinkler heads or covers or hang any objects from the head. Be aware that if the drywall is removed from the ceiling, such as in repair or remodel, plastic sprinkler pipes could melt because they would be exposed directly to a fire.
- ✓ If a gap exists between the cap of a concealed sprinkler head and the ceiling, do not caulk it. In the event of a fire, the cap is designed to fall off so the head can spray. Caulking will impede this action.
- ✓ Have the fire sprinkler system professionally tested annually (or more frequently if required by the local fire authorities) to determine that the system will operate as designed in the event of a fire.

Telephone

General Subject Information: Telephone wiring in homes today can range from a simple two-pair wire system to a complex, high-tech fiber optic system for voice and data transmission. The wiring of the telephone system within the house is likely to be done by a specialty contractor hired by the builder and not by the company providing the telephone service. The telephone service comes into the house in a box called the *interface*, located on an outside wall. The company providing telephone service takes responsibility from the street to the interface, and homeowners take responsibility from the interface throughout the inside of the house.

Recommended Use and Maintenance:
- ✓ Be careful when performing any aftermarket alterations to the house telephone system. After market alterations may affect the performance of the original wiring.

Satellite or Cable TV

General Subject Information: Television signals are received by most households today through satellite dishes or cable TV. Cable TV, or CATV, is the acronym for Community Antenna Television. Like the telephone system described in the previous section, there is an *interface* on the outside of the house. The cable service provider or satellite dish provider takes responsibility for the quality of the signal to the interface; from the interface throughout the house is the responsibility of the homeowner. It is most likely that a specialty contractor working for the builder installed the cable wiring within the house. A simple system is run directly from the interface to the wall outlet. A more complex system involves a panel within the house and an amplifier that boosts the signal to the various rooms in the house.

Recommended Use and Maintenance:
- ✓ Be aware that the addition of aftermarket splitters, boosters, and other cable enhancing devices may cause the system not to perform as originally intended, and also may void any warranties.
- ✓ Be certain that any holes drilled into your house to mount a satellite dish are completely sealed with a long life caulk. The same recommendation applies at the penetration through the exterior wall of the satellite cable bundle.

Chapter Eight

G R O U N D S

includes:

Drainage

Landscaping

Irrigation

Retaining Walls

Fencing

Grounds

General Subject Information: Water must be kept away from foundations in order to reduce the potential for structural and interior damage. Not only can seeping water cause interior damage, it can cause the foundation to move. There are several potential causes for seeping water: 1) lack of gutters and downspouts (downspouts should be piped either to the street or away from the foundation, see **Chapter 5 "Gutters and Downspouts"** section); 2) lack of required slope away from the foundation; and 3) overwatering landscaping near the foundation. All three of these causes can be mitigated with proper and vigilant use and maintenance.

Drainage

Comments: Keeping water away from the foundation is one of the most critical responsibilities of a homeowner. When water has an opportunity to pond (stand), it can lead to severe interior damage to both finishes and furnishings. Water vapor can migrate through concrete as well as through cracks in the soil beneath the foundation. All "soils" must maintain a minimum vertical distance of 6 inches from finish floors/any portion of the wood floor that is subject to decay, to top of finished soil. The 6 inch distance can be reduced to 4 inches if the surface that surrounds the foundation is a hard surface.

Any water that is standing or ponding within 6 feet of the foundation should dissipate within 24 hours after a rain. Under extreme weather conditions, ponding or standing water may take longer to dissipate. Water that stands or ponds under extreme conditions is considered normal.

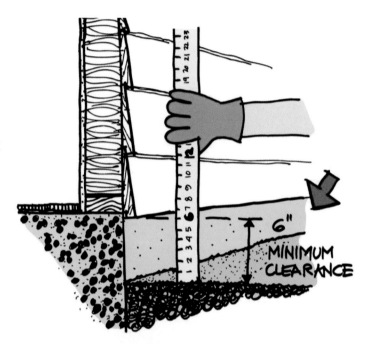

SEPARATION BETWEEN WOOD AND SOIL
(USE CARE WHEN INSTALLING PATIOS AND DECKS)

Recommended Use and Maintenance:

✓ Always maintain the required slope away from the foundation. It is advisable to check slope requirements with the local building department, since some cities and counties require slopes to be more than 2%. This means that the soil next to the foundation will be at least 1/4 inch higher than the soil one foot away from the foundation.

✓ Be especially careful (1) during the installation of landscape materials, where the existing grade could be modified by leveling it out, causing either a *negative slope* or a flat slope, or (2) when hiring a landscape company that modifies the grade during soils preparation and planting, also causing either flat or negative slope.

✓ It should also be noted that if gutters and downspouts are not installed, you may want to consider installing them yourself or having a qualified and licensed expert install them for you. If downspouts are installed, the water should discharge onto approved splash blocks or into a pipe collector system and never towards the foundation.

✓ Keep all *swales*, *sump pumps*, and drains free of silt and other debris.

✓ Repair any erosion that occurs during a rainstorm. **NOTE**: *If you modify the existing grades that surround the foundation this may cause the soils to subside.* You are responsible to monitor and correct this condition.

✓ Yard drains should be flushed with a garden hose prior to the start of the rainy season and should show evidence of free flow at the curb or at the sump (if applicable), or at other parts of discharge into a storm system.

✓ If the house is equipped with a subterranean drainage system around the foundation or through the foundation, the cleanouts (if applicable) of this subdrain should be flushed twice a year. There should be evidence of free-flow through the curb or into the sump. Clogged drains can be cleared with a rooter machine or high pressure water jets.

Landscaping

General Subject Information: The addition of landscaping is a significant and positive amenity to any individual house or housing project. The care taken in the initial installation of landscaping and proper maintenance afterwards are essential in keeping the property looking well kept and attractive.

Comments: Typically, trees, shrubs, and ground cover have different warranty periods. Common grounds of large developments that have a Homeowners Association should have a start-up maintenance schedule with their independent maintenance company, followed by a standard yearly maintenance schedule thereafter. Even after applying *pre-emergent* weed control, it is still virtually impossible to guarantee against some weed growth in planted areas.

Recommended Use and Maintenance:

✓ Maintain the soils by periodically adding the proper amount of nutrients, i.e. fertilizer, mulch, humus, and minerals required for the particular type of planting.

✓ Supply the required maintenance to ensure that the plants stay healthy. Do not overwater the plants. Any water that is standing (*ponding*) 30 minutes after watering is a sure sign of overwatering. If there are no specific instructions as to the proper maintenance of the subject plants, then you should consult an expert, i.e. nursery, or a licensed landscape maintenance contractor. All plants, shrubs, sod and trees should be maintained properly to ensure the healthy growth of the plants. These recommendations also apply to Homeowner Associations, where applicable.

✓ Provide proper maintenance regarding weed control. This may include application of pre-emergent herbicides, spot spraying of contact weed killers and hand weeding.

Irrigation

Comments: Particular attention should be taken regarding sprinkler head location. Water should not spray directly onto building walls, masonry, metal and wood fencing. Some landscape professionals recommend drip irrigation at the foundation perimeter.

Recommended Use and Maintenance:

✓ Be sure not to overwater the landscape. Ponding or standing water that accumulates at and around foundations can cause serious structural damage, insect infestation, and plant root rot. Adjusting the watering times on the irrigation controller to avoid overwatering is an important maintenance item. In Homeowners Associations (HOAs) where landscape maintenance would most likely be performed by a professional service, overwatering can be commonplace. Steps should be taken to prevent overwatering by individual homeowners and by HOAs.

✓ Regularly check all sprinkler heads to make sure that they do not spray towards the structure.

✓ Change the backup battery of the landscape irrigation controller or clock (if the controller has one) once a year.

✓ If the irrigation system is not needed for seasonal use, turn it off and winterize it. **See "Winterizing Your Home" in the Introduction.**

DO NOT ALLOW IRRIGATION WATER TO SPRAY AGAINST HOUSE WALLS AND FENCES.

Retaining Walls

General Subject Information: The most prominent material used in retaining wall construction is CMU (*Concrete Masonry Unit*) block. Pressure treated wood can be used for low height retaining walls. If a retaining wall fails, water is generally the biggest catalyst for failure. There are two ways that water attacks retaining walls: (1) surface water and (2) sub-surface water. Surface water should be directed into concrete **swales** or **brow ditches** to a proper drainage area. Subsurface water should be diverted through a sub-drainage system, i.e. trench drain, and directed to a proper drainage location.

Cement products can and often do crack. However, walls that are designed to retain soil or gravel may have some form of a **waterproofing** product applied to the side of the wall that is against the hillside. Along with a waterproofing membrane, a protection board is also often applied to protect the membrane from damage when soils are placed against it. A swale or berm is often utilized in order to transfer surface water away from the wall. In order to remove any sub-surface water from the hillside, a **trench drain** or weep holes are generally used as a vehicle for subsurface water removal and removed via a pipe to a designated location. Some walls, notably the loose block variety (blocks not held together with mortar), are designed to have ground water pass through the joints.

Comments: Minor wall cracks are generally considered normal, as long as there is no dislocation of the plane of the wall and no vertical dislocation. Cracks should not be left open to the weather. They should be filled with an epoxy, have epoxy injected into them, or be filled with expansive set grout.

Efflorescence is a white chalk-like powder that appears as a result of moisture migrating through the mortar, dissolving salts within and leaching to the surface. Salts in the brick or block itself may also cause efflorescence. Another cause of efflorescence is a high alkaline content in the cement.

RETAINING WALLS

HELP PREVENT SOIL MOVEMENT

Recommended Use and Maintenance:

✓ Maintain the method for surface water to be diverted away from the wall either through a concrete **swale** or **berm**.

✓ Try to identify where the trench drain (providing that one has been installed) **daylights** (daylight refers to the end of the drain pipe that is visible) in order to determine whether or not the drain system is clogged during heavy rains. Check and flush the drainage system before the rainy season starts.

✓ Repair minor cracks in the concrete in a timely fashion. Cracks should be filled or injected with an epoxy, or with expansive set grout.

✓ On long slopes that are relatively steep, surface water should also be diverted away from the top of the wall to prevent conditions that could lead to cracking.

✓ Efflorescence is easily removed by brushing or by a high-pressure water spray.

✓ Do not build something on top of the wall or alter the slope in a way that would compromise the design of the wall.

Fencing

Comments: The useful life of a fence can be greatly affected by proper or improper use and maintenance. By not maintaining adequate clearance between fence-to-finished grade, the useful life of the fence may be drastically reduced.

True wrought iron fences are seldom installed today. What is referred to as "wrought iron" is really square or round tubular steel. Because the tubes are hollow, they can be more susceptible to rust at the welds. Any fence will need regularly scheduled maintenance in order to maximize the full *useful life* of that fence. There are many different factors that play a part as to how often the fence needs maintenance, such as:

→ Site-specific location of the fence—is it located in an area of direct harsh sunlight or is it in a wet and shady area;

→ Type of material—metal, wood or masonry;

→ Is there a finish or not—stains, sealers, paint;

→ Geographic location—coastal, desert, inland, or mountain environments.

Recommended Use and Maintenance:

✔ Do not change the finished grade in any way that would affect the intended clearances between fencing and soils.

✔ If natural conditions (i.e., rains wash soils down onto the fence) cause the clearances to change, you should make the appropriate corrections.

✔ Planting shrubs whose foliage is in constant contact with the fence may also reduce the life of the fence boards.

✔ Bottom rails and pickets or side boards should maintain a minimum clearance of two inches to finished grade.

✔ Do not allow irrigation sprinklers to spray directly onto the fence. Check sprinkler heads throughout the season to make sure they have not become turned.

✔ It is recommended to paint or seal a wood fence every three years. This should prolong its useful life.

✔ Wrought iron gates and fences should be inspected semi-annually and painted whenever rust is evident, particularly at the base of all posts.

✔ Keep the fence in good repair by periodic renailing of loose boards.

✔ Gate latches should be lubricated annually and hinge and latch screws tightened.

✔ Stucco fending (patio fencing) should be inspected every spring. Cracks on the top of the fence should be caulked and repainted and fence post bases should be checked for dryrot.

✔ The condition of wood fences should be inspected every spring. Look for nails that have backed out of boards, fence posts that are leaning and kick boards that have rotted. All leaning posts should be straightened, all loose boards should be renailed and all rotted kick boards should be replaced.

APPLY OIL BEFORE
HINGES RUST AND BIND.

Chapter Nine

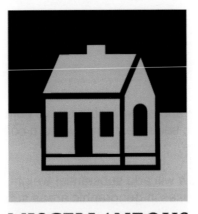

MISCELLANEOUS

includes:

Ice and Snow

Noise Transmission

Mold and Mildew

Septic Tanks

Smoke Detectors

Wood Destroying Insects

Radon

Miscellaneous

Ice and Snow

General Subject Information: Ice and snow problems are common to a large portion of North America. Homes in the deep south, southwest, and western coastal regions are not frequently confronted with ice and snow issues.

Comments: Accumulations of snow will add substantial weight on the structure of a house, particularly to roofs and decks. Houses in geographic areas subject to snow are built to accommodate these additional loads. However, storms may exceed normally predicted ranges, producing excessive snow accumulations. During periods when heavy snow and icing occur, access doors, garage doors and even windows can be blocked. Reasonable protection includes overhangs and orientation away from customary storm exposure.

When snow melts and then re-freezes, ice may form dams at areas such as roof eaves and deck perimeters. Subsequent melting or rainfall can accumulate behind the dams, and the depth of resulting ponds can exceed the height of waterproofing systems. When this happens, water can enter the interior of roof and wall systems causing damage. In addition, ponded water on flat roofs and decks can exceed the design loads for these components of the house. All of these conditions can be greatly reduced or mitigated with proper maintenance and use.

Recommended Use and Maintenance:

✓ During periods of exceptionally heavy snowfall, it is likely that accumulations of snow will have to be removed from the roof. Except in isolated areas, there are companies that perform this service. Do not allow accumulations of snow or ice to remain on the roof for long periods of time.

✓ When garage doors, access doors and windows become blocked, you should take preventive measures to keep repetition of these problems to a minimum.

✓ Become aware of the causes of ice dams and the preventive steps that can be taken. Keep gutters, drains, deck openings and major catch basins free of debris and other obstructions.

✓ If there are publicly owned drainage facilities nearby that are subject to blockage, do not hesitate to contact authorities to request maintenance. Failure to do this could result in localized flooding during periods of rapid snow melt, with consequent property damage.

✓ Refer to **"Winterizing Your Home" section in the Introduction** for more details.

Noise Transmission

General Subject Information: Attached housing typically has common walls (called party walls) and floor / ceiling assemblies that are common to neighboring units. This subject applies to attached housing only. Single family detached homes are not included in this section.

Comments: To prevent sound transmission between adjoining units from exceeding the Sound Transmission Coefficient (STC), walls must be assembled in accordance with industry accepted cross-sections (for example, those published by the Gypsum Association), or their established equivalents. Prior to granting a building permit, the Building Inspection Department checks the floor and wall design to see if it meets an approved design standard. Most issues of noise transmission are subjective issues of individual tolerance to noise. There are a few steps that homeowners can take to limit additional noise problems. ***Refer to Recommended Use and Maintenance below***.

Recommended Use and Maintenance:

✓ Avoid any changes that affect the assembly of sound-insulating party walls or ceilings; avoid making new openings in walls and floors.

✓ Do not install a stereophonic speaker system in or on the ***party walls*** of a townhouse or condominium.

✓ Do not drill into or create holes in party walls.

✓ You are living in a type of housing where some noise transmission between units is inevitable. Be considerate of your neighbors.

✓ Carpets and similar sound-absorbing floor materials reduce noise transmission to units below.

✓ If you wish to install hard flooring in your home (tile, parquet, etc.), be sure to consult with your builder representative about the use of sound-absorbing underlayments.

Mold and Mildew

General Subject Information: Mold and mildew (fungi) and the ***spores*** by which they reproduce are present everywhere in the environment, including indoor air and surfaces of buildings. Usually the small numbers of these tiny organisms do not cause any problems. However, high levels of moisture combined with organic materials provide conditions that can result in their rapid growth. In high concentrations, some of these fungi may consume wood and other building materials sufficiently to cause decay and rot. Others may produce stains and unattractive coatings on interior and exterior surfaces. Some people can develop allergy-like symptoms if exposed to mold. While it is quite difficult (if not impossible) to entirely eliminate these organisms in normal residential environments, control of interior humidity and preventions of leaks limits their growth and minimizes any resulting affects.

There are thousands of types of molds and mildews. A limited number of varieties are commonly associated with damage to buildings. Under conditions favorable to growth, these fungi can form dense colonies that may be visually unattractive. Of all the known varieties of mold and mildew, only a few are believed to pose health hazards. Among these few are "*stachybotris chartarum*" which can produce toxic mycotoxins. In the few varieties of mold and mildew that are believed to produce adverse health effects, concentrations must be relatively high to affect most healthy individuals. It is important to note that at the present time, there are no accepted federal, state, or local health-based standards for permissible exposure to mold and mildew. Nevertheless, whether it is believed that the potential for ill affects is little or large, it is universally accepted that houses should be kept as free from mold as possible.

Some common areas for mold and mildew growth in the typical residential environment are: 1) around window frames where condensation or leaks occur if the residence is tightly sealed, inadequately ventilated, or if the temperature is colder outside than inside; 2) at and near toilets, sinks, and tubs (anywhere water splash and leaks are likely to occur); 3) in basements and other spaces which are below ground level, when drainage and/or waterproofing of walls is not adequate, or is failing due to age or lack of maintenance; 4) anywhere two or more pieces of wood are tightly fitted together, and water can get between them (typical examples are unflashed wood trim around windows and doors, wood railings and caps with open miter joints, and failure to maintain caulking in these areas); and 5) in poorly ventilated and damp enclosures.

Sometimes mold will grow in enclosed (not visible) locations, such as the cavities at exterior walls. If the building construction or lack of maintenance allows water to leak into wall cavities, mold can grow in the affected areas. Resulting damage can progress unseen for some time. Aside from gray or black stains and blotchy patches that are readily identifiable as mold, signs that should help identify some potential problems include softness in drywall, water stains at walls and ceilings, damp carpets, buckling or swelling of exterior surfaces, and a persistent musty odor. These are *possible* indications and do not prove that mold or mildew exist. The actual existence of mold and mildew must be established by visual observation and in some cases, by appropriate testing and expert inspection.

Recommended Use and Maintenance:
Familiarize yourself with strategies to identify, minimize, and prevent mold growth. Watch for and eliminate condensation on walls, around windows, and other cool places. Indoor humidity should be kept low by proper use of ventilation devices. Generally, a relative humidity of 60% or less should limit condensation-caused mold. The following are thirteen essential Maintenance and Use Recommendations for mold and mildew.

1. Vacuum and clean regularly. Use mold-killing products while cleaning bathrooms.

2. Use air conditioners and dehumidifiers, especially in hot, humid weather. Clean dehumidifiers often. Empty them daily or have the appliance drip directly into a drain.

3. Vent clothes dryers to the outside.

4. Keep attics and crawl spaces ventilated and insulated.

5. Clean refrigerator drip pans regularly according to manufacturer's instructions.

6. Inspect and maintain air conditioning and heating systems on a periodic basis. Clear out or repair the condensate line if the air conditioner's drip pan overflows.

7. Promptly dry any damp or wet indoor areas. This includes shower stalls and tubs.

8. Always use vent fans in baths, kitchens, and laundries. Keep the vent fan running for 15 to 30 minutes after use of room to ensure condensation is adequately removed. Open windows whenever possible.

9. If mold or mildew begins to grow around the edges of window frames (due to condensation), remove it promptly with a detergent / water mixture and a disposable rag.

10. Establish/maintain roof drainage into gutters and downspouts. Maintain the ground slope away from the house foundations.

11. Repair leaks as soon as they are discovered. Keep in mind that mold can grow within 24 hours after the start of a leak. Proper homeowner inspections and prompt maintenance are essential.

12. Do not store organic materials (such as paper, wood, cardboard, books or clothes) in damp locations.

13. If the house experiences a flood or sewer overflow, make sure that all affected areas are cleaned up thoroughly and promptly.

You should seek help if you are concerned about possible indications of mold and mildew. Some sources for help include biology departments of major universities, city and county health departments, and the organizations to which health and hygiene specialists belong, such as the American Conference of Governmental Industrial Hygienists (ACGIH). This group can be contacted through their website: **http://www.acgih.org**.

For more detailed information, try these web sites:

> US Environmental Protection Agency – http://www.epa.gov
> Centers for Disease Control and Prevention – http://www.cdc.gov
> California Department of Health Services - http://www.dhs.ca.gov
> Illinois Department of Public Health - http://www.idph.state.il.us
> New York State Department of Health - http://www.health,state.ny.us
> Oregon Department of Human Services - http://www.ohd.hr.state.or.us
> Washington State Department of Health - http://www.doh.wa.gov

→ **IF MOLD AND MILDEW IS SUSPECTED TO EXIST, THE MOST IMPORTANT THING TO DO IS TO STOP THE SOURCE OF WATER, IF POSSIBLE, AND TO NOTIFY THE BUILDER IMMEDIATELY.**

Comments: Prevention and elimination of leaks is discussed in other sections of this Manual (See Chapters on Walls, Roofs, Exterior Components and Utility Systems). Nevertheless, where leaks *do* occur, it is possible that mold and mildew may follow. If mold and mildew are present as a result of leaks, the repair of leaks should include removal of materials that are stained, coated or otherwise adversely affected by such organisms. Because removal of moisture can arrest the growth of these organisms and because surfaces that are not significantly damaged can be cleaned or treated, it may be possible to retain some or all affected building components during the repair process. In severe cases, removal or retention of building components is a technical matter that is best handled by a specialist in mold and mildew. The specialist will determine the molds and mildews present and the best way to remove them.

Most of the molds and mildews that appear around window frames and doors, in tile grout at tubs, showers and kitchens, as well as other interior locations, are the result of inadequate maintenance or improper use. At times interior humidity may rise sufficiently so that moisture condenses on cool surfaces (such as windows, doors and walls). These conditions provide a fertile environment for the growth of molds and mildews, which most frequently appear around window and door frames, and at joints between frames and surrounding drywall and wood trim. Because of their warm and moist conditions, shower stalls and tub surrounds are also ideal places for mold and mildew to grow. Most of these conditions are controllable through appropriate use and maintenance of the house.

The appearance of mildew or fungi on outdoor siding may result from three principal sources: 1) leaks that allow water to enter between the siding and the material behind the siding; 2) an environment that is excessively damp, shady and lacking in air circulation; and 3) condensation of moist air on interior surfaces.

Mildew or mold should not be allowed to remain in the heating and ventilating systems. The problem usually results from moisture getting into the ductwork, either from a leak or condensation. Improperly insulated ductwork can also be a cause. It may be difficult to identify the presence of mold or mildew in ductwork, although a musty odor can be an indicator.

Recommended Use and Maintenance:

✓ Promptly address any instances of leakage, report to the builder any instances of leakage, so that preventive repairs can be accomplished before significant damage occurs. If leaks are corrected quickly, mold and mildew may not flourish, and repairs and clean-ups are much easier to accomplish.

✓ Showers and tubs should be routinely cleaned and towel dried after each use.

✓ Window frames and joints should be periodically cleaned in order to prevent mold and mildew growth.

✓ If mildew or mold is observed, use a mildewcide (available at cleaning supply or hardware stores) to prevent any regrowth.

✓ It is helpful to air out rooms on a frequent basis.

✓ Ensure that all exhaust fans and other air circulation devices are functioning properly and used routinely. Windows should be open or vent fans should be operating at all times while showering or bathing. Allow fan to run 15 to 30 minutes after showering or bathing.

✓ Do not install air deflectors over heat supply grills.

✓ Open draperies often during rainy periods to allow air to circulate around windows.

✓ Limit the use of atomizers or humidifiers.

✓ Window tracks and *weep holes* should be cleaned at least twice yearly to prevent mold and mildew.

✓ Keep siding sealed and painted. Avoid spraying siding and stucco with landscape sprinklers.

✓ If mold and mildew grows on outside walls, take prompt action. Use of mildew-killing sprays and brushing with water and soap can arrest or reverse mildew conditions.

✓ Avoid planting shrubbery that will block sunlight and ventilation from siding. Do not allow ivy or other vine plants to grow on siding and keep existing shrubbery pruned back from siding.

✓ Notify the builder promptly of any suspected problem of this nature.

Septic Tanks

General Subject Information: A typical private waste system works in the following manner: waste is piped out of the house into a watertight holding tank. There, bacteria break the waste down into solids, liquid and scum. The sludge settles into the bottom of the tank, the scum rises to the top, and the liquid flows into 1) a distribution box where then channeled through perforated pipes that leach out into a field of loose gravel, known as the leach field, or 2) to a separate pit through solid pipes.

Comments: Under certain conditions septic systems can fail or overflow as a result of saturated leach lines, freezing, change in water tables, or excessive use of plumbing fixtures. Use of high phosphate detergents and overuse of detergents can result in leach field failure.

The odors that come from a septic tank are largely affected and controlled by use and maintenance. A septic tank that is overused (beyond its capacity) or one that has not been regularly pumped out will become quite odorous.

Recommended Use and Maintenance:
- ✓ The tank should be pumped out every 2-3 years, depending on the size of the system and the number of people that live in the household. The local health department may require more frequent pumping.
- ✓ Keep the tank pumped out on a regular basis. Periodically add a bacteria-enhancing agent which can be found at hardware stores. If the number of persons using the system increases, consider expanding the system.
- ✓ The following items are examples of improper use regarding septic tanks, and all are to be prevented and avoided:

  - ☒ DO NOT pour paint thinners, pesticides, motor oils, or chemicals down drains or in toilets.
  - ☒ DO NOT dispose of grease, fat, paper towels, or feminine sanitary products in toilets.
  - ☒ Use drain cleaners <u>with caution</u> and sparingly (drain cleaners kill bacteria that break down sewage).
  - ☒ DO NOT use dyed toilet tissue (dyes are harmful to the bacteria in the tank).

Smoke Detectors

General Subject Information: According to nearly every city or county ordinance or by adoption of a fire safety code, smoke detectors are required to be installed in specific rooms in a residence, interconnected with each other, and maintained in an operating condition. New installations of smoke detectors must be wired to the house electrical system as well as having a battery operated back-up. If one smoke detector alarm sounds, all should sound.

Comments: Smoke detectors are designed to be smoke sensitive; this is for the protection of the occupants. In all likelihood when smoke detectors sound at the time of cooking, the room has been overloaded with cooking vapors. If the detector sounds each time a fire is built in the fireplace, there may be a ventilation problem (See **Chapter 6 "Fireplaces"** or **Chapter 5 "Chimneys and Flues"**).

Recommended Use and Maintenance:
- ✓ Operate fireplaces and cook in a manner that does not cause undue quantities of smoke to be generated within the house.
- ✓ Test detectors once a month using the test button on the detector.
- ✓ All newly installed detector systems operate both off the house wiring and battery back-ups. Make sure the batteries are changed on a regular basis so the back-up system will function in the event of a power failure.

TEST SMOKE-DETECTORS MONTHLY

Wood Destroying Insects

General Subject Information: Wood destroying insects can either feed on, nest in, and otherwise invade a house. They cause significant unseen damage when allowed to flourish. These insects can enter the structure through the soil from furniture or other wood items brought into the home or by flying into the structure. Once inside the house, these insects most often will feed on wood or wood products and cause damage. The most important methods of preventing and controlling wood-destroying insects are preventative maintenance and periodic inspections. Homeowners can perform both of these tasks. It is important that you become aware of the conditions that invite these insects into the home and learn to recognize the signs of insect infestation. If you are unsure about signs of infestation, consult a licensed pest control company to perform a professional inspection.

Comments:
There are five common species of insects that can invade a house or other wood structure:

1) **Subterranean termites** – Subterranean termites travel from the soil into the wood framing members of the house. Indicators of the presence of subterranean termites are mud tubes in the soil through which they enter the house. These mud tubes can run up the concrete foundation or be free standing like soda straws. Another sign of subterranean termites is what appears to be "bubbles" on interior wall paint. This occurs as a result of termites eating the paper from the drywall inside the house.

2) **Dampwood termites** – Unlike subterranean termites, dampwood termites do not travel via mud tubes. Instead, dampwood termites get into the house by boring into damp wood materials. Any part of the wood structures that are in direct contact with the earth, such as attached fencing, wooden porch steps and landscape dirt piled up against the siding provide a direct route into the house for dampwood termites. These locations are where the termites colonize and continue to feed on the wood. Locations of common dampwood termite infestation also include areas near plumbing leaks or wood members with excessive moisture. Indicators of dampwood termites are difficult to recognize, since the openings through which they enter a structure are often sealed with wood products. The two best ways to detect dampwood termites are: 1) annually probe wood pieces that are close to the earth with an ice pick, or 2) have an annual termite inspection from a licensed pest control company.

3) **Drywood termites** – Drywood termites are flying insects and can be introduced into the home through open windows and doors or through vent openings. Drywood termites can also enter the house through cracks or openings in the foundation or siding and trim. Drywood termites become detectable as they emerge by flying away from the wood. Further signs of these termites are the small emergence holes that are slightly larger than a thumbtack hole.

4) **Wood boring beetles** – Wood boring beetles are also flying insects that can invade a house via open windows, doors, or through vent openings. These insects and similar beetles feed on floors, cabinets, and furnishings, as well as other wood materials. Another way wood boring beetles can enter a house is from items brought into the home, i.e. cabinets, furniture and picture frames. This is especially common if the items are from overseas. Indications that wood boring beetles may be present in a house or in a wood product are the

emergence holes. These holes can range from the size of a pinhead to the size of a pencil eraser. You should carefully inspect all furniture to make sure there are no emergence holes. If emergence holes or little piles of sawdust are observed, hire a licensed pest control company to perform an inspection.

5) **Carpenter ants** – Unlike the other insects mentioned, carpenter ants do not actually feed on wood products. Instead, they create tunnels and galleries inside wood members and then nest inside. Carpenter ants commonly enter a house from shrubs that are growing against the house or from tree branches that closely overhang the structure. As the ants travel through wood, they make a network of tunnels that can weaken the internal structure of wood. If a carpenter ant infestation is large enough, the structural integrity of the house may be compromised and significant structural damage may occur. Indicators of carpenter ants include piles of wood shavings, typically with small insect parts within the shavings.

Recommended Use and Maintenance:

Exterior –

IT'S TIME TO CALL A PEST CONTROL COMPANY!

- ✓ Periodically inspect all exterior siding for cracks. Seal cracks with a good 25+ year caulking to keep the siding watertight. Be sure to include wood trim, eave openings, and fascia boards in this inspection and maintenance routine. Twice a year, inspect interior and exterior foundation and basement walls for termite tubes.
- ✓ Make sure there is a waterproof membrane between any installed planters and the house walls. If the planter is wood, it should have a metal lining, and it should be raised off the deck or patio with spacers.
- ✓ Make sure concrete patios or decks are installed with a 2% positive slope directed away from the house. If the patio or deck is poured too high, water can be drawn back up into the siding causing decay and providing a route for termites to enter the house.
- ✓ Avoid attaching to the house any wood that has direct contact with soil. This includes patios and decks. Any wood that has direct contact with or is near soil by 6 inches should be pressure treated.
- ✓ Do not nail or otherwise attach any part of a fence to a house wall, unless a metal termite shield is installed between the exterior of the house and the fence.
- ✓ Always store firewood away from the house in a structure or holder that is not in contact with the ground.

Interior –
- ✓ Never place any wood or cellulose (paper, cardboard, certain fabrics, or actual wood products) on crawlspace soil or basement floors. If you want to use this area for storage, have a concrete or masonry barrier installed between the soil and storage surface. Always elevate the stored material from the soil or slab by 6 inches using bricks or concrete blocks. Inspect semi-annually for termite activity.
- ✓ Make sure the crawlspace / basement area receives proper ventilation. Do not block any vents.
- ✓ Keep all plumbing in proper repair and do not allow leaks to go unrepaired. This is also a good practice to prevent mold.
- ✓ In garage areas, avoid storing materials over a *control joint* (the joint intentionally cut in concrete slabs to control where concrete cracks). If this area is used for storage, periodically move the items and inspect for signs of infestation. Termites can travel through cracks between concrete and through the control joint-foundation wall intersection.

Radon

General Subject Information: Radon is a naturally occurring radioactive gas that is a result of decaying radium and uranium. Radon typically comes from rocks containing uranium, like certain granites or shales. This colorless and odorless gas can be found in the air or it can be absorbed into ground water and then subsequently released into the air. Radon is considered to be chemically inert, that is to say it does not readily combine with other chemicals. However, certain levels of radon exposure can be hazardous to human health.

Why is it important to know about radon?
Radon is classified as a human carcinogen by the Environmental Protection Agency. However, any cancer resulting from inhaling radon is not likely to become apparent for at least 20-30 years after initial exposure. The level and duration of radon exposure and use of tobacco (smoking) are factors in determining the risk of developing lung cancer. Exposure to radon does not result in acute respiratory symptoms such as colds, asthma, or allergies.

A standard unit of measurement for radon is picocuries per liter of air (pCi/L). In the United States, the average level of radon found indoors is 1.3 pCi/L, but can range from 0.25 to over 3,000 pCi/L. There is insufficient data to define a "safe" or harmless level of radon, though it is accepted that the greater the level of exposure and the longer duration of exposure, the greater the health risk. The EPA guideline states that radon levels should not exceed 4 pCi/L indoors. If the radon level of your home measures above 4pCi/L, you should consider a radon mitigation system.

Comments: Radon gas enters the home through the soil from cracks and openings in concrete slabs, crawl spaces, floor drains, sumps, and concrete blocks. Generally, living areas that are closest to the soil will have the highest levels of radon, as compared to living areas or rooms on second stories. Since radon can be absorbed into the ground water from radon contaminated soil, it can also be present in tap water. Radon present in water can be released when showering, washing dishes, or washing clothes. Radon can also be present in water when the water source is a well that is exposed to uranium and radium rock strata. Radon is of more of a concern when it comes from this type of source.

Recommended Use and Maintenance:

Radon mitigation is not a federal law requirement but it is required in some states. Homeowners may decide to reduce the level of radon in the home at their own discretion.

- ✓ If a homeowner is concerned about radon levels in his or her home, a passive radon detector can be obtained. Always follow the manufacturer's instructions to obtain accurate results and to interpret those results correctly.
- ✓ Homeowners may also consult a government agency for assistance with determining the amounts of radon present in the home and any recommended subsequent actions.   To get more information on radon testing, call **1-800-SOS-RADON**.
- ✓ A water test should be considered, especially if the indoor air levels of radon are at or above the EPA guideline of 4pCi/L. The water company that supplies the house should have information about the source of the water and any radon tests performed. If the house has water supplied by a well, homeowners should contact a laboratory certified for radon testing to perform a water test.
- ✓ For more information on radon, refer to **www.epa.gov**.

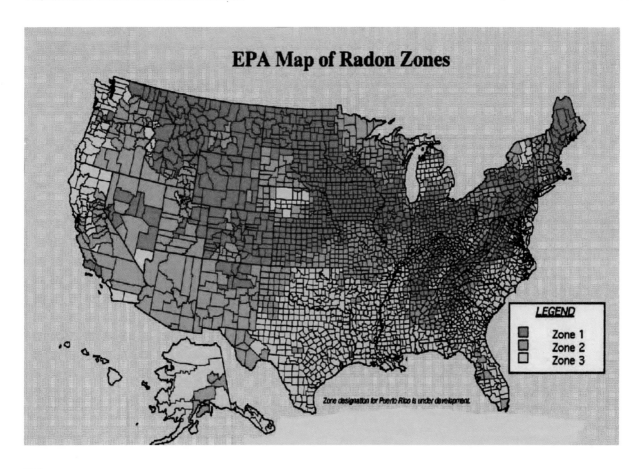

EPA Map of Radon Zones

Zone designation for Puerto Rico is under development.

LEGEND
Zone 1
Zone 2
Zone 3

Zone 1 states have a predicted average indoor radon screening level greater than 4 pCi/L (red)

Zone 2 states have a predicted average indoor radon screening level between 2 & 4 pCi/L (orange)

Zone 3 states have a predicted average indoor radon screening level less than 2 pCi/L (yellow)

This map, from the US Geological Survey, is to be used as a guide and reference. This map should not be used to determine a homeowner's actual risk of radon exposure or to determine actual radon levels in a home. Homeowners should consult a government agency or certified laboratory to determine the actual radon levels in their home, or within the region they live. Additional maps can be found on **www.epa.gov**.

Homeowner Maintenance Summary

The following list summarizes minimum maintenance requirements that you should perform, along with the tear-out maintenance schedule. For more specific details, each maintenance item is referenced to a section within the Manual. All maintenance work should be done either by you, if you are experienced and comfortable performing the maintenance, or by a maintenance person who is experienced and insured. A maintenance person who holds a contractor's license is typically better qualified. If you are interested in performing your own maintenance, many local home improvement stores offer classes and instructional seminars.

→ **Bathroom Caulk.** The caulk joints in bathrooms need to be inspected and re-caulked every six months. This includes the joint at the bottom of the shower, the joint between the tub and the wall, the joint where the tub or shower pan meets the floor, and vertical inside corners and seats. It is very important that these joints do not pass any water; otherwise dryrot can accumulate progress unseen for years. Refer to **Chapter Seven: Plumbing** for additional details. Joints should be cleaned of old caulk before re-caulking. Any mold or mildew found growing in bathrooms (or other places in the house) should be removed immediately with a mildewcide available at most home improvement stores. The cause of the mold or mildew should be discovered and the cause eliminated.

→ **Ceramic Tile Grout.** Regrout or color caulk all cracks after the first year. Once the house frame reaches equilibrium (in less than two years), regrouting or caulking should not be required. Tile grout should initially be sealed with a silicone based sealer and thereafter every two years. Refer to **Chapter Six: Countertops** for additional details.

→ **Chimney Cleaning.** The chimney flue should be professionally cleaned every two years if there are more than 50 fires per year or if two cords of hardwood (like oak) or one cord of softwood (like pine) are burned, subject to any restrictions or requirements of the manufacturer. **Refer to Chapter Five: Chimneys and Flues** for additional details.

  → **Doors.** Patio sliding doors should have their tracks (bottom sill) swept and vacuumed monthly. The weep holes should also be inspected and cleaned as needed. Dust and dirt build-up in slider door tracks will interfere with the proper operation of the small wheels that the doors slide on. For swing doors, the hinges and latches should be lubricated annually with a dry lubricant specifically made for locks and latches.

→ **Drains**

  ✓ **Deck**. Deck drains should be flushed with a garden hose and should show evidence of free-flow prior to the start of each rainy season. **Refer to Chapter Five: Decks** for additional details.

  ✓ **Yard**. Yard drains should be flushed with a garden hose prior to the start of the rainy season and should show evidence of free flow at the curb or at the sump (if applicable). **Refer to Chapter Eight: Drainage** for additional details.

✓ **Subdrains**. If the house is equipped with a subterranean drainage system around the foundation or through the foundation, the cleanouts (if applicable) of this subdrain should be flushed prior to the start of the rainy season. There should be evidence of free-flow through the curb or into the sump. **Refer to Chapter Eight: Drainage** for additional details.

→ **Drywall**

✓ **Cracks**. Minor cracks in drywall usually appear within the first 12 months of occupancy. These cracks typically occur around doorframes, cabinets, and window frames and can be easily caulked. **Refer to Chapter Six: Plaster and Drywall** for additional details on cracks and proper maintenance and use.

✓ **Nail Pops**. Nails will sometimes back out of the drywall as the frame of the house dries out. This is not a structural problem, but the nails should be redriven and the heads should be spackled and painted with touchup paint. **Refer to Chapter Six: Plaster and Drywall** for additional details.

→ **Electrical**

✓ **GFIs**. Ground Fault Interrupters should be tested monthly. When testing, press the **TEST** button and the RESET button will pop out. Push in the RESET button to restore the circuit. If the GFI will not reset, it may be faulty or there may be an open circuit. Contact a qualified, licensed electrical contractor to check the circuit. **Refer to Chapter Seven: Electrical** for additional details.

✓ **Closet Ceiling Lights**. Light bulbs in the closets must be covered with a lens or globe as part of the fixture. When changing bulbs in the closet light fixtures, do not exceed the manufacturer's recommended wattage for the bulb requirement, and do not leave the fixture cover off. Lights left on in closets can generate a significant amount of heat and become a fire hazard. **Refer to Chapter Seven: Electrical** for additional details.

✓ **Aluminum Wiring**. While most household wiring is copper, the larger wires (known as cables), are likely to be aluminum. All wires are covered with insulation. Aluminum cables are often used to provide power to air conditioners, heat pumps, electric clothes dryers, and electric ovens. Aluminum is a softer metal than copper. Over time it can deform, or "creep", where it is connected. When aluminum creep occurs, the connection is no longer tight and sparking jumps through the gap. Appliances will consume more power and breakers will trip. It is recommended that the terminal connections of aluminum cables be inspected and tightened if necessary by a qualified, licensed electrical contractor within the first two years after occupancy. **Refer to Chapter Seven: Electrical** for additional details.

→ **Fencing**

✓ **Wood**. The condition of wood fences should be inspected every spring. Look for nails that have backed out of boards, fence posts that are leaning and kick boards (at the bottom) that have rotted. All leaning posts should be straightened, all loose boards should be renailed and if the kick boards have rotted significantly, they should be replaced. **Refer to Chapter Eight: Fencing** for details.

✓ **Wrought Iron**. Wrought iron gates and fences should be inspected four times a year to check for rust, particularly at the base of all posts. If rust is discovered, it should be scraped away and the section should be painted with rust-resistant touchup paint. **Refer to Chapter Eight: Fencing** for additional details.

✓ **Stucco.** Stucco fencing (patio fencing), should be inspected annually at springtime. Cracks on the top of the fence should be caulked and repainted and fence post bases should be inspected for dryrot. All dirt should be removed from the fence post bases. **Refer to Chapter Eight: Fencing** for details.

→ **Furnace Filters.** If the house has both heating and air conditioning, the furnace filters should be changed at least every six months or according to the filter manufacturer's recommendation. If the house has heating only, the furnace filters should be changed prior to the winter season. If the house is exposed to considerable wind driven dust, the above filter change schedule should be doubled. **Refer to Chapter Seven: Heating** and **Chapter Seven, Cooling** for details.

→ **Garage Doors**

✓ **One Piece**. One-piece garage doors (doors that raise and lower as one single piece) with automatic openers or garage doors without automatic openers should be lubricated at the hinge points every six months with 30w oil. The keepers (the long threaded rods that run across the top and bottom) should be kept tight to prevent the door from sagging in the middle.
✓ **Sectional**. Sectional doors (doors that roll up into the garage ceiling on tracks) should have the track rollers lubricated with 30w oil annually.
✓ **Automatic Opener**. The automatic openers, whether they are chain drive or screw drive, should have the drive mechanism (chain or screw) lubricated with a light grease annually.
✓ **Bolts**. Garage doors vibrate while opening and closing. Therefore, it is important that an inspection be made every six months for the first year and annually thereafter for bolts that can be wiggled or moved by hand. All loose bolts should be tightened. **Refer to Chapter Five: Garage Doors** for additional details.
✓ **Weatherstripping**. Check flexibility and contact with floor.

→ **Gutters and Downspouts**. Gutters and downspouts should be cleaned and flushed twice annually. The first task is performed just prior to the rainy season and the second time during the rainy season after the trees have shed their autumn leaves. Note that certain trees, such as pine and eucalyptus, shed throughout the year and require more frequent maintenance. Prune branches that overhang roofs and gutters. **Refer to Chapter Five: Gutters and Downspouts** for additional details.

→ **Pest Control**. Insects, particularly termites and carpenter ants, can be harmful to the structure of the house. An annual inspection should be made of the foundation (both on the outside and inside of the crawlspace). Look for brown termite tubes running up the foundation walls and bore holes of the carpenter ants on the exterior of the house. Do not hesitate to call a pest control service if destructive insects are believed to be present. Firewood should be stored away from the house in a structure or holder that is not in contact with the ground. Do not let vines grow on the house as they attract insects. Unwanted roosting birds, such as pigeons, starlings and swallows, should be removed by a licensed pest control company. **Refer to Chapter Nine: Wood Destroying Insects** for additional details.

→ **Irrigation Sprinklers.** Irrigation sprinklers should be checked annually at the beginning of the growing period (usually March or April) to be sure that the heads are clean and do not spray against the house and that the sprinkler lines have not broken during the winter. Spray patterns should also be checked during the growing season. **Refer to Chapter Eight: Irrigation** for additional details. During the rainy season, irrigation controller times should be changed frequently to avoid overwatering and flooding.

→ **Locks**. Once a year, or when they become stiff, apply a dry lubricant as directed into the lock. Use a lubricant specifically designed for locks and avoid use of popular synthetic oil sprays. The latter can form a gummy residue on lock parts.

→ **Sink Traps.** Depending upon frequency of use, sink traps should be cleaned with a cleanser approved for the type of plumbing pipes under the sink (plastic or metal). For a kitchen sink that receives daily use, a cleaning every 60 days should be sufficient. DO NOT put sink cleaner into a garbage disposal. It may corrode the cutting blade edges.

→ **Solid Surface Countertops**. Do not apply countertop surface enhancers or cleansers such as Pledge™ or 409™ to a new solid surface countertop. These products will only attract and hold discoloring items such as coffee, wine or catsup to the surface. The new nonporous, bacteria-free solid surface countertop will remain in good condition if it is simply wiped off with a soft sponge or cloth, with an ammonia based product such as glass cleaner. For integral solid surface sinks, use a mild abrasive such as Softscrub™ to cut any grease or discoloring buildup that has accumulated on the surface of the sink. Clean off any harsh chemicals such as nail polish remover as soon as possible. Do not cut directly on the solid surface countertop or slide any rough edged objects across the countertop, since these items will create surface scratches in almost any type of countertop. To prevent shocking the surface of any type of sink, do not pour extremely hot grease or water into any sink without simultaneously running cool water. Do not place extremely hot items (such as sheet pans from a 450 degree oven) directly on the countertop or sink. **Refer to Chapter Six: Countertops** for additional details.

→ **Trim and Siding.** The term "trim" refers to the wooden trim either abutting the stucco or placed on the wooden siding around windows and doors. Trim should be inspected each year prior to the start of the rainy season; and if trim is pulled away from the house or caulking has deteriorated, these areas should be re-caulked. If warping or twisting is severe (more than ½ inch), the trim should be replaced. Refer to **Chapter Six: Moldings and Trim** for additional details. Do not caulk the <u>bottom</u> gap of the trim piece <u>over</u> a window or patio door. Also, the siding (exterior wall material such as panels, lap boards, shingles or other non-stucco, non-brick or non-stone material) should be inspected for warpage and protruding nails. Inspections should be annual and prior to the start of the rainy season. Warpage should be caulked and painted, and protruding nails should be pulled and replaced with a slightly larger nail. Use hot dipped galvanized box or common nails in exterior applications. Drive the nail head even with the siding; DO NOT drive the nail head into the siding. Driving the nail head into the siding may break the seal and cause the siding to swell and leak during precipitation. Touch up all work with caulk and paint.

→ **Vents.** This includes kitchen hood filters and bathroom laundry fans. The hood filters should be removed and washed with a grease removing cleanser at least 4 times a year (depending upon use). Bathroom and laundry fans should be vacuumed with a hose vacuum and crevice tool at least once a year.

→ **Water Heater.** To prolong the life of the water heater, accumulated sediment should be removed from the heater tank once a year. This task can be performed by attaching a thick wall garden hose to the drain spigot at the bottom of the tank and draining out <u>no more</u> than two gallons. **Since the water being drained is very hot, be very careful that the hot water does not come into contact with persons, animals, plants, or any material that could be damaged by scalding water (120 degrees F to 160 degrees F).**

→ **Windows (includes Patio doors).**

✓ **Seals**.　Inspect for broken or breached window seals in dual pane windows at least annually.　Windows with broken or breached seals are easily identified by having a moist, foggy, or filmy condition between the two panes of glass.　When this condition exists, the insulating value of the window is greatly diminished. The only repair is to replace the glass. **Refer to Chapter Five: Windows and Patio Doors** for additional details.

✓ **Weep Holes**.　The weep holes at the bottom of windows and patio doors serve a purpose: to allow water to drain out from the track during rainstorms. Weep holes should be inspected at least annually to make sure that no debris has plugged the holes and that rainwater will drain freely from them.　**Refer to Chapter Five: Windows and Patio Doors** for additional details.

✓ **Tracks.**　The tracks of windows and patio doors should be swept and vacuumed frequently to prevent dust and debris buildup. Clean window and door tracks to allow the sliding vent to move more freely, so that the water draining through the weep holes will not be impaired by wet debris.

HANDY HAMMER

CONGRATULATIONS ON A JOB WELL DONE

<u>Maintenance Notes:</u>

RECOMMENDED PERFORMANCE MAINTENANCE

RECOMMENDED MAINTENANCE SCHEDULE							
MAINTENANCE ITEM	**PURPOSE**	**FREQUENCY**	**DIFFICULTY**	**DATE PERFORMED**			
AIR CONDITIONER	Start twice during winter months; keeps mechanical parts from sticking. Service professionally	2Y Y4	● ◆				
BATHROOM CAULK	Seal joints that are subject to being wetted; prevent leaks, dry rot, mold and mildew.	2Y	▲				
CERAMIC TILE GROUT	Seal grout with silicone based sealer; cracked grout should be caulked with a caulk specifically made for filling grout. Improves appearance, prevents leaks.	Y	■				
CHIMNEY CLEANING	Remove build up of tar and creosote from the flue; prevents flue fires.	Y2	◆				
DECKS	By inspecting deck surfaces for cracks in coating, loose boards and surface sealers, minor maintenance and repairs extend deck life.	Y	●				
DOORS	Vacuuming tracks and lubricating hinges and latches keeps parts smooth.	M/Y	●				
DRAINAGE	Keep drain from backing up and flooding during the rainy season. Make sure debris is removed from ditches and swales. Maintain positive drainage away from buildings.	Y	●				
DRYWALL (CRACKS AND NAIL POPS)	Set nails, caulk and paint. Improves appearance of finished interior wall surfaces.	Y	■				
ELECTRICAL (GFI TEST)	Safety of electrical circuits. Test GFI circuits (kitchen, bath, garage and outdoor) monthly.	M	●				
EXHAUST FANS	Vacuuming accumulated dust from bathroom and laundry fans for proper air flow.	2Y	●				
FENCE (INSPECTION AND REPAIR)	Retains privacy and security. Prolongs life of fence. Wrought iron schedule is 4Y.	Y	■				
FURNACE FILTER CHANGE	Helps remove dust and pollen from interior air; improves furnace efficiency; less energy consumption.	2Y	●				
GARAGE DOOR SYSTEMS	Lubrication promotes smoother, less noisy operation; extends systems life. Tighten keepers to avoid sag on one piece doors.	2Y	●				
GARBAGE DISPOSAL	Fill with ice and operate. Cleans and sharpens.	Y	●				
GROUNDS	Inspect for pavement breaks, heaving sidewalks and tree roots, dry rot at decks and blockage of drainage system. Avoids more expensive repair costs.	Y	■				
GUTTERS AND DOWNSPOUTS	Prevent overflow onto walls; prevents eve leaks; extends gutter life.	2Y	●				
INSECT CONTROL	Detected and treated early will prevent structural damage; controls annoying pests. If found, treat monthly.	Y	▲ ◆				
IRRIGATION SPRINKLERS	Direct water spray properly. Eliminate excess watering, staining of exterior walls and dry rot of structures.	2Y	■				
KITCHEN EXHAUST HOOD	Wash kitchen hood grease filters in the dishwasher.	Y	●				
ROOF INSPECTION / MAINTENANCE	Detect and correct conditions that can lead to leaks and premature roof replacement. Be sure to read Chapter Four to learn the process for inspection and repair.	Y	■ ◆				
SINKS	Inspect under sinks in kitchen, bath and laundry/utility for leaks. Early detection avoids greater damage and expensive repair. Clean sink traps to avoid backups and plugged drains; promotes sanitation. Use only cleaners recommended by manufacturer. Clean faucet aerators to maintain water flow.	4Y	●				
SMOKE DETECTOR	Replace batteries for safety and keep clean.	Y	●				
TRIM SIDING AND STUCCO	Caulking and painting keeps system water tight; improves appearance, extends major maintenance periods; reduces chance of mold and mildew. Paint all exterior wood trim, siding and stucco.	Y	◆				
WATER HEATER (PARTIAL DRAIN)	Extends water heater life; provides more efficient operation; uses less energy.	Y	■				
WINDOWS (TRACKS AND WEEP HOLES)	Keep windows sliding freely. Avoid water standing in tracks and potential leaks.	2Y	■				
WINDOWS (SEALS-DUAL PANE)	Appearance, broken seals reduce insulating ability. Replace when foggy.	Y	◆				

KEY

FREQUENCY:
Weekly = W   Twice a year = 2Y   Every three years = Y3
Monthly = M   Four times a year = 4Y   Every four years = Y4
Yearly = Y   Every two years = 2Y   Every six years = Y6

DIFFICULTY:
● Easy, no special skills required.
■ Some skill required.
▲ Good idea to get instruction on this item from a local improvement store.
◆ This task should be performed only by a qualified professional.
Refer to Homeowner Maintenance Summary for additional details.

Glossary

A glossary of terms is an important tool for each homeowner. Like almost every trade or profession, the homebuilding industry has, throughout time, developed a language all its own. Many of the industry used terms such as "heart, stud, cricket, jack, apron and chase" have completely different meanings in everyday life. While it is not possible to list all of the homebuilding terms and their meanings here, the ones most likely to needed by a homeowner are defined below.

ABS-black plastic pipe used to carry waste water (sewage) from the various drains in the house to a pipe known as the soil pipe. The soil pipe is located just outside the foundation of the house. ABS pipe is also used as plumbing vents through the roof.

ANSI-the acronym for American National Standards Institute. This is an organization that tests building components and determines if the components meet certain prescribed standards.

ASHRAE-the acronym for American Society of Heating, Refrigerating, and Air-conditioning Engineers. This Association establishes standards for heating and cooling, among other things.

Aggregate-a mixture of small smooth rocks; an ingredient used in making concrete.

Air handler-the specialized fan inside the furnace or air conditioner that blows warm or cold air through ducts to the rooms.

Anchor bolts-bolts that hold the frame of the house to the foundation. Anchor bolts, also known as J-bolts, are cast in the wet concrete of the foundation during the concrete pouring process to secure the mudsill.

Apron-the small strip of trim wood that is underneath the windowsill. The windowsill is known as a stool in the homebuilding industry.

Attic-the space in the house between the ceiling of the top floor and the underside of the roof. The attic needs to be insulated over living areas and vented to allow proper air circulation from the house in the summer and winter. Most houses have an interior attic access panel which can be located in the ceiling of a hallway, closet or bedroom, and allows access to the attic.

Backsplash-a part of the countertop in a bathroom and/or kitchen (and sometimes laundry room) that is a vertical piece of countertop material connected to the wall. A backsplash is typically 4 inches to 6 inches in height.

Baluster-the posts that support the handrails, located on the sides of stairs. The posts where the handrails start or stop are called the newell posts.

Barge board-a board attached to the edge of a roof that projects beyond the wall of the house (also referred to as barge board).

Batten-a strip of wood or plastic (usually 1 inch x 2 inches) that is applied to a roof to hold the concrete or clay tiles in place. Also, a batten is a strip of wood used to cover the joints of panels of exterior siding.

Beam-a horizontal piece of lumber that is used to carry part of the weight of the house. Beams are found at the roof, between floors, and between the basement or crawl space and the first floor.

Berm-a mound of dirt that is placed in landscaped areas to control the flow of storm water. Berms are also used in landscape beautification, to break up flat areas.

Bird stop-a metal, plastic, or wood insert found at the lowest point of a tile roof (typically the round or barrel shaped tiles). This is to keep birds and other creatures from nesting in the underpart of the roof.

Bleed through-a term that describes a material that passes through another material and generally discolors the second material. An example of bleed through is redwood and cedar wood sap (tannins) that bleed through paint. It can also apply to rust from nails and staples that bleed through stucco.

Blocks-pieces of wood installed at the ends (and sometimes at intermediate points) of floor joists, as to prevent the joists from twisting. By the use of blocks, the floor joists are tied together to create a more rigid component. Blocks are also found where floor joists lap one another (the joists cannot span the entire distance so a lap is created). Blocks are also used between studs to serve as a firestop. The blocks are typically made from the same material as the joists or the studs.

Breaker-a specialized switch found inside a panel (usually gray and known as a breaker panel) that will interrupt the flow of electricity in the event of a short circuit or an electrical surge. The act of interrupting is called "tripping". The small handle of a tripped breaker will be in the middle position between the markings OFF and ON. A tripped breaker will have to be turned off before it can be reset to the ON position. Breakers are usually found in groups in the panel and they are labeled as to which circuits they control.

Brow ditch-a ditch that sits on top of a retaining wall. It is designed to keep surface water from flowing behind and over the wall.

Building Official-the person who is the head of the local department that issues building permits. This is usually a county or city agency. Building Officials, through their deputies, perform inspections and enforce the various Building Codes.

Building paper-a specially made thick paper that is stapled to the outside of the frame of the house. Building paper is used prior to application of the exterior finish material (such as stucco, wood siding and shingles). The paper is impregnated with a substance during its manufacturing process that makes it resistant to the flow of moisture. If the stucco or siding leaks, the building paper will serve as a secondary backup to prevent moisture from getting into the walls.

Bull nose-a piece of material that projects slightly past the supporting material and is rounded at its outer edge. Bull nose pieces can be found on roofing, interior trim, stair tread and countertops and "finish off" a flat surface.

Capillary action-the act of drawing a liquid, usually water, into another material. A good example of this is a sponge absorbing water. In the building industry, water can be drawn up into wood, stucco, or concrete by capillary action.

Casing-known as trim pieces that will finish off an opening. Most commonly found at door openings and mistakenly called frames, but casings can also be found around windows and shadowboxes.

Caulk-a gooey material that is used to seal joints for the purpose of keeping water out. Caulk is usually found around bathtubs and is applied with a tool known as a caulking gun. There are many different types of caulks for various uses. It is critical to use the correct variety of caulk product for each situation.

Cement-a term that has been mistakenly interchanged with the word concrete, but in fact is one of the ingredients of concrete. Cement is the "paste" that will bind sand and aggregate together. Because of its chemical composition and alkalinity, cement can burn the human skin.

Chain drive-the mechanism that opens and closes the garage door and is part of the automatic garage door opener. These automatic garage door openers operate with three types of drives, either chain drive, screw drive, or belt drive.

Chase-a chase is a horizontal or vertical box in which a flue pipe, generally a chimney flue, is located. The chase is built around the flue and it extends above the roofline by an amount specified in the Building Code. Chases can also contain plumbing pipes or wiring.

Cleanout-an opening in a plumbing waste line to allow access to the piping for the purpose of inspection and cleaning. Cleanouts are required by the plumbing codes and are typically found beneath kitchen sinks and just outside the foundation of the house.

Closed loop system-any system that uses the same fluid or gases over and over and is returned to the source for heating or cooling.

Coffered ceiling-a ceiling that is not flat but has a portion of it lifted up to create a more dramatic architectural effect. The lifted portion is usually found in the middle of the ceiling.

Common area-areas that are owned in common by all members of a homeowners association. This term is associated with condominium projects and planned unit developments. Included areas are the exterior of buildings, landscape, driveways, recreation facilities and mailboxes. Common areas usually have their own legal description located in the deed to the condominium or individual lot, as applicable.

Compaction-an engineering term given to the degree of tightness of the soil around and under the house or behind a retaining wall. The soil under the foundation must achieve a certain degree of compaction before the foundation can be poured. Driveways, patios and walkways should be poured on compacted soil. Uncompacted soil is often referred to as native soil or loose soil.

Compressor-a motor driven pump that compresses a gas as part of the air conditioning process.

Concrete-a mixture of sand, gravel (sometimes called aggregate) and cement. This mixture becomes concrete when it is mixed with water and is allowed to cure.

Condensate line-the plastic or metal pipe that comes out of the air conditioning part of the furnace. Condensate lines conduct water from the air conditioner coil to the outside of the house or to a trap.

Condominium-buildings, parts of which are owned in common with other people. This is a legal term and is often confused with an architectural style. Condominiums can include townhouses, flats and even detached homes, so long as part of the project is owned in common by all of the owners of the project.

Control joint-a linear separation made during the pouring of concrete or stucco made by troweling with a v-shaped tool. Its purpose is to provide a slightly weaker spot in the concrete so it will crack along the joint. The joint can also be a groove made with a concrete saw within one day after the concrete is finished.

Corbel-a bracket having at least two sides at right angles and often ornately carved. This bracket may support a shelf or an element that projects out from a house such as a bay window or a fireplace mantel.

Corner bead-a corner bead is a long strip of material that is applied vertically to "finish off" a corner. The corner may be a drywall corner or a stucco corner. Corner beads are usually made of metal, including wire, and sometimes are even made of stiff paper.

Counter-flashing-metal flashing that fits up under the visible flashing on roofs, around chimneys and windows.

Crawl space-this is the space between the soil and the underside the first floor joists. It is found in houses that have a pier and grade beam foundation, and do not have a basement. The Building Codes specify the minimum height of the crawl space.

Cricket-a section of the roof that is often found between the roof and a vertically projecting structure, such as a chase. The cricket is constructed to deflect water away from the chase, where the chase and the roof meet. This is so that water does not accumulate and leak into the house.

Crowning-a condition usually applied to wood, often hardwood floors, where the wood takes on moisture and the center portion of the board becomes higher than the edges. The opposite of cupping. This condition can also apply to floor joists, where the center of the joist becomes higher than the ends.

Crown molding-a decorative architectural trim piece made of wood, plastic, plaster, or foam that covers the intersection of walls and the ceilings.

Cupping-a condition that occurs when boards (including flooring) dry unevenly and the edges become higher than the center.

Cure-the act of a building material drying out and coming to equilibrium with its surroundings. A good example of curing is concrete. Concrete cures from the initial placement as it dries out. In the first three days concrete is very weak and after 28 days concrete, when properly mixed, is said to reach 90% of its maximum strength. Other materials that cure are stucco, paint, deck coatings and fireplace linings.

Damper-a hinged flap of metal found above the firebox in fireplaces to close off the flue to warm air escaping from the room when there is no fire. The damper must be open when using the fireplace. It also prevents wind from blowing down the chimney when it is not in use. Dampers are also found in the ducts of heaters and exhaust fans.

Daylight-a term given to a condition where a covered or buried object protrudes through its cover and becomes visible. An example is the visible end of a buried pipe—at the point where the pipe becomes visible, it is said to have "daylighted".

Displacement-refers to any horizontal or vertical movement of a building or the component within. More frequently it is used to describe the settlement or the heave of a foundation and the settlement of utility trenches that were once level with their surroundings.

Door-a movable structure used to close off an entrance to a room, building or covered enclosure that consists of a panel of wood, glass, metal or other various building materials. An entire glossary could be written about doors, but here is a condensed version:

❑ **Exterior door-**any door that is on the outside wall of a house. The door has been manufactured to be weather resistant subject to proper maintenance.
❑ **Fire rated door-**a door that has been rated by an independent laboratory and has a label attached setting forth its rating. These doors can be made of many materials including wood, fiberglass, steel and composite wood material. A 20-minute fire-rated or 1 3/8 inch solid core door is generally required to be placed between the garage and house and sometimes the entrances to condominium homes. The rating usually states that the door will withstand a fire for a certain number of minutes.
❑ **Flush door-**a door that has a front and back panel (also known as the skin) that is perfectly smooth with an adjoining wall.
❑ **French door-**a door or series of doors that are hinge mounted (as opposed to a patio door that moves on tracks) and provides access to a courtyard, patio or garden. French doors are often found with divided lites (small panels of glass in individual frames as opposed to one large panel). May also be used as interior doors between rooms.
❑ **Hollow core door-**refers to the method of construction of that door. These doors have an airspace between the front panel and the back panel of the door. The airspace between the front and back panel often contains a cardboard "honeycomb" inside.

- **Interior door-**any door that is found inside the house and may include doors from one room to the other as well as cabinet doors.
- **Overhead door-**also known as the garage door. May be constructed as a one-piece door or constructed in sections. A sectional door rides up into the garage ceiling on tracks whereas the one-piece door operates with springs and hinges.
- **Patio door-**an exterior door that is usually comprised of two panels, one sliding and one stationary. Patio doors are also known as sliding glass doors.
- **Pocket door-**a door that does not swing in or out, but slides across the opening from a "pocket" inside the wall.
- **Raised panel door-**a door that is manufactured with panels either individually inserted into the door or embossed into the face of the door as part of the manufacturing process. Raised panel doors can be solid core or hollow core.
- **Shower door-**the glass or plastic door that permits access to the shower.
- **Solid core door-**a door that has no airspace between the front and back panel, but is instead solid wood or some material that is glued or laminated to the front and back panels. Used in exterior applications and more custom interior applications.

Doorstop-the piece of trim that is put around three sides of a door jamb to stop the movement of the door when it is closed and sometimes to provide a rudimentary seal for light, noise and air.

Downspout-a specialized pipe usually made of aluminum, galvanized steel or plastic that runs from the roof gutter opening down the wall to the ground.

Draftstop-material that is inserted into a wall to limit the spread of fire and smoke. Frequently used materials are wood, drywall, insulation and masonry block. Draftstops are also found in chimney chases and between floors of multi-story condominium units. They are usually made of sheetmetal.

Drain:

- **Deck drain-**a drain located in a patio or elevated deck to control and direct rainwater in that area.
- **French drain-**similar to trench drain, but there is no pipe at the bottom of the trench.
- **Overflow drain-**an overflow drain protects the structure in the event that the main drain plugs up. The overflow drain is typically two inches higher than the main drain. Overflow drains are also found on bathtubs and lavatory sinks.
- **Plumbing drain-**any drain that is found at the low point of the plumbing fixture, such as a bathtub, shower or sink.
- **Roof drain-**any drain that drains the roof area including the hole in the gutter. If the drain is at the edge of a flat roof, it is called a scupper.
- **Trench drain-**a drain often located in a yard or hillside area that consists of a trench with a perforated pipe at the bottom and gravel filled on the top. The term is incorrectly interchanged with french drain.
- **Yard drain-**also known as an area or site drain. This drains rainwater and irrigation run-off from landscaped areas.

Draw-the ability of a flue, chimney, or vent to pass air, smoke, or other vapors from the bottom up and out the top. Unless impeded by some source, all vertical tubes have a natural draw due a difference in atmospheric pressure.

Drip irrigation-a method of irrigating plants, shrubs and trees with low pressure, low volume piping and tubing system. The advantage of drip irrigation is that it significantly conserves water compared to conventional methods of irrigation.

Dryrot-refers to a rotting condition usually involving wood but sometimes paper and drywall. When the material is wetted repeatedly and dries between wettings, dryrot occurs. Wood that is dryrotted is internally infected by a fungus. The wood will often look almost in its original form, but it will have no structural value and can be easily pierced with a screwdriver.

Drywall-a gypsum based panel that is nailed or screwed to the studs that makes up the interior wall of the house. These panels are also known as Sheetrock®. Drywall derives its name from being a dry process as opposed to the wet lath and plaster process that was used years ago to finish off interior walls. Drywall is typically finished by placing tape over the panel joints and applying drywall compound, known as taper's mud, and finishing the process by spraying or troweling drywall texture onto the wall.

Dual pane-a term given to the construction of a window, skylight or patio door. Dual pane means that there is an outside layer of glass and an inside layer of glass separated by a spacer up to 5/8 inch in thickness and a dead air space between the two panes of glass. This is sometimes called insulating glass.

Dutch gutter-a rainwater diverter found on roofs, often over doorways or where the placement of a conventional gutter is impractical. It is usually inserted between rows of shingles or tile, and protrudes above the roofline by about three or four inches.

EIFS-an acronym for Exterior Finish Insulating System. This component system, when applied to the exterior of a house, consists of building paper, foam insulation, wire mesh (lath) and a synthetic stucco product.

Eave-the underside of a section of the roof that extends past the walls of the house.

Efflorescence-white powdery material that appears on the surface of concrete and stucco as the drying out process occurs. Wet winter weather may cause concrete and stucco to effloresce.

Elastomeric-a term given to coatings that have "stretch" characteristics and are applied to many decks and low-pitched roofs. Elastomeric components are mixed together and applied with trowels or rollers. Several coats are applied and if the surface is to be walked upon, often sand, pebbles or crushed walnut shells are applied in the final coat. Some elastomeric paints are made to be applied to stucco.

Escutcheons-a piece of trim, chrome, brass, plastic or wood that is used to finish off the area of penetration of a pipe through a wall or ceiling. They are usually round and one inch to three inches in diameter.

Expansion joint-a cut that is made or a gap that is deliberately left between sections of building materials to allow for expansion and contraction of those materials. Examples of expansion joints are found in large expanses of stucco walls, concrete driveways and garage slabs, and in swimming pool decks and patio decks. Expansion joints that are trowelled into concrete when it is poured are also called control joints. Since concrete frequently cracks, the cracks are supposed to occur at these joints to control the cracking from occurring elsewhere.

Exposure-a roofing term that measures (usually in inches) the amount of roof shake, tile or shingle that is exposed to the weather.

Fascia-the trim board that covers the edge of the rafters at a pitched roof. May also be incorporated with a gutter to collect rainwater from the roof.

Filter fabric-a textile made of synthetic threads that allows water to pass through but prevents soil particles from passing through. Used to wrap underground drainage pipes and are placed underneath roadways in unstable soil areas.

Finish coat-refers to the final coat of material to be applied to a house. Examples are stucco, paint, drywall texture, deck coatings and other materials that require more than one application before being complete.

Firebox-that portion of the fireplace where the fire is actually built.

Firestop-these are very similar to draft stops in their location and purpose. Firestops are placed between floors, between walls, in vent shafts, in soffit ceilings, and in chimney chases to retard the spread of fire.

Flapper valve-the rubber or plastic valve at the bottom of the toilet tank that keeps the water in the tank until the flush lever is pushed.

Flashing-strips of metal material that are used to direct water and wind from one surface to another. Flashing is placed where a roof and a wall intersect and around the intersection of chimneys and roofs. It is also placed where roof planes come together and where trim pieces often protrude from walls. Walls that terminate without being under a roof, such as a parapet, are flashed with cap flashing. Sometimes two flashing components work together by one piece of flashing sliding underneath the other. This is known as counter-flashing.

Flatwork-a broad-based term referring to concrete placement that is flat. Examples include driveways, patios and walkways.

Flue-the pipe protruding from the top of the firebox, furnace, water heater, or other gas fired appliance that carries the hot burned gases to the atmosphere and outside the house.

Flush-to be in the same plane or level with another object.

Foundation-the lower most structural element of the house that supports the weight of the house. There are two primary foundation types: the raised footing and the slab on grade. There are also several variations of the two primary foundation types:

- **Basement-**these foundations are a form of grade beam foundation, since the basement wall becomes the grade beam. Basement walls are founded on perimeter footing and a slab is poured between the footings to complete the basement floor.
- **Conventional slab-**this refers to the method of reinforcing a building slab. Steel bars, called rebar, are crisscrossed to form a mat over which concrete is poured. In some cases, the reinforcing may be welded wire mesh.
- **Footing-**a term given to the underside of the grade beam or the underside of the edge of a slab. To provide additional foundation stability, foundations are made wider than the grade beam itself, and deeper than the thickness of the slab.
- **Grade beam-**concrete is poured in a form to allow a first floor framing of the house to occur at least 6 inches higher than the surrounding ground. The grade beams comprise the exterior perimeter of the house and sometimes the interior grade beams are also poured to support bearing walls.
- **Piers-**are holes drilled into the ground typically between 6 and 18 feet deep, reinforced with steel rods known as rebars, and filled with concrete. Piers are typically connected to the underside of grade beams. Less frequently, piers independently support the underside of houses. Even less frequently, piers are connected to the underside of slabs where unstable soil conditions warrant them. The purpose of a pier is to provide additional stability to a foundation against upward and downward pressure.
- **Post tension slab-**a method of reinforcing where cables are crisscrossed in the slab area prior to pouring concrete. After the concrete is cured, the cables are tightened under extreme tension to provide a tight and dense foundation.
- **Slab on grade-**where the concrete is poured on top of the finished and prepared lot that is ready to receive the concrete. Hence the concrete slab becomes the first floor of the house. Slab foundations can also have grade beams poured underneath them.

Frame-is the skeleton of the house. It contains the elements to support the weight of the house and defines the shape of the house. The frame and the foundation are the most important structural components of the house.

Furnace–a mechanical device located in, around, or under the house, or sometimes in the attic, that is powered by either gas (natural or bottled), electricity, or fuel oil or a combination of sources of power. The furnace provides a source of heat for the house.

Garage door-see Doors, garage.

Grade-a term denoting the elevation of a particular lot above sea level and the degree of levelness of that lot. Finished grade is the elevation of the lot (sometimes known as the pad) after the grading operations have been completed. A slab on grade is a foundation that has been poured on the finished grade. Grade is also a term used to describe the type, quality, and strength of lumber that is used in the frame of a house.

Grain-the lines of harder and darker wood that run though the field of a piece of lumber.

Greenboard-a special type of drywall that has moisture resistant characteristics. Its common application is basically seen around tubs and showers. Typically, it is either green or blue in color.

Ground fault interrupter-a special electrical breaker that is more sensitive to electrical changes than standard circuit breakers. Areas that are subject to moist or wet conditions such as kitchens, baths, garages, and outdoor areas must have their electrical outlets connected to a ground fault interrupter.

Grout-material which contains cement, sand, or a plastic polymer material and a coloring agent, that is placed between pieces of tile or marble. The joints between pieces of tile or marble are called grout joints. Stonework can also be grouted. Grout is also used to fill voids under foundation sills.

Gusset-a triangular piece of material often made of wood, plastic, or metal used to strengthen intersecting corners. Gussets are used inside hollow core doors and inside cabinet frames.

Gutter-an open linear collector and distributor of water. Gutters may be found at the eaves of roofs or can be associated with curbs and sidewalks in streets and parking areas. Another possible location for gutters is in the middle of driveways and streets.

Gypsum-a powdery mineral that is white in color, non-combustible, and is the primary ingredient in indoor plaster and drywall.

Gypsum board-see drywall.

HVAC-the acronym for Heating, Ventilation and Air Conditioning. Refers to the specialty work of contractors who install furnaces, fans, air conditioning systems and sometimes other sheet metal items such as flashing, gutters and downspouts.

Hardboard-a general term used to describe a variety of simulated wood products that are used primarily as exterior siding.

Hard water-water that has a high mineral content and consists mainly of calcium and magnesium compounds. Hard water restricts soap from lathering, and it can form deposits inside water lines and water heaters.

Header-a structural framing member made of wood or steel that spans the opening over a window or door.

Heart (Heartwood)-a term referring to the grade of lumber, usually redwood. Heart wood is from the inner core of the tree trunk. It is considered the best lumber because it is more uniform in appearance. The opposite of heart wood is sap wood. The term "sap wood" refers to the lumber that is milled from the outer-most portion of the tree. Sapwood is usually lighter in color than heartwood.

Hold-downs-structural metal straps embedded in the foundation at the time of pouring concrete and are then nailed to the framing members during construction. Hold-downs can also be comprised of anchor bolts, threaded rods, and metal gussets to tie the frame to the foundation in the event of an earthquake or loads (forces) caused by wind.

Holidays-small areas that the painter has missed or covered very lightly. Derived from the saying, "It looks like the painter took a holiday."

Impermeable-a term which describes the ability of a material to resist the passage of liquid through it. A plastic sheet or membrane that does not allow the passage of water considered impermeable. Semi-permeable membranes allow for the passage of some moisture.

Insulation-a material used in the home building industry that keeps a house from either gaining or losing heat. Normally insulation is put into the walls, under the bottom floor, and into the attic space during construction. Sometimes insulation is placed on the outside of slab foundations and is attached to the outer face of the studs before applying the exterior finish.

Interface-a point where two or more functions interact. For example, the telephone service company wiring meets and interacts with the house telephone wiring at a box called the interface.

Jack-has four meanings in home building. The first refers to the metal assembly on the roof through which the plumbing vents and furnace flues run. The jack may be a combination of metal and a rubber gasket to ensure a watertight seal. The second use of the term jack refers to a screw device that can remedy certain out of level conditions on foundation and floor frame members. The third definition applies to a "phone jack", or the wall plate into which the phone cord is plugged. The fourth refers to any short filler in roof or wall framing such as "jack rafter" or "jack stud".

Jamb-the stationary component of a door assembly to which the hinges are attached. The door assembly (excluding the door itself) is comprised of a jamb, stop, and casing.

Joist-the horizontal members of the house frame that are the most common elements of a floor or ceiling system. While joists are the most common element of the floor system, other horizontal members known as beams or girders can also make up the floor system. Common joists have one nominal dimension, typically at 2 inches and the other nominal dimension at 8, 10, 12, or 14 inches, depending upon how far they span. It is common practice today to use a manufactured component as a joist. This is called a truss; it is comprised of wood, metal or a combination of both. If a truss is used, it has been manufactured in a factory and approved for use by a structural engineer.

Knocked down-a style of finished wall texture that is applied coarsely with a texture spray gun. The bumpy surface is then "knocked down" with a large metal straight edge known as a texture knife.

Latch-the portion of the doorknob assembly that protrudes out from the door and upon closing the door fits into the hole provided by the strike. The term can also generically refer to any part of a door, gate or opening mechanism that hooks into a receptacle designed to receive it.

Lath-a material to which plaster is applied. Lath is usually metal in the form of wire or mesh and is applied over building paper to the exterior of the house prior to plastering. The lath provides a surface for the plaster to hang onto during its wet application. Lath reinforces plaster much in the same way rebar reinforces concrete. Prior to the wide spread use of drywall, interior house walls were plastered with gypsum plaster. The lath used behind this type of plaster were long strips of wood.

Leaf-a term given to the section of a door that swings in or out with another companion door, and which does not close into a jamb on the strike side. Good examples are french doors that connect to one another when closed.

Ledger-a horizontal piece of lumber or steel used to support joists and rafters. The wood ledger, which is at least 2 inches nominal thickness, may support the joists by having them sit on top of the ledger or hang from the face of the ledger by metal brackets known as joists hangers. The most common application for the ledger is in the construction of a deck attached to the outside of the house.

Membrane-a thin sheet of material used to prevent the passage of water or water vapor into an area that would be damaged by water. Often used under deck surfaces.

Millwork-refers to house components that are generally part of the interior finish of the house, and which are manufactured in a mill or shop, rather than constructed at the site of the house. Examples of millwork are cabinets and doors.

Miter cut-a method of cutting wood (usually trim pieces) at an angle other than 90 degrees so as to conceal the joint when the pieces of wood are placed together. Corner pieces of trim such as door casings and baseboards are often miter cut so that the cut end is not visible.

Mortar-mortar is a mixture of sand and cement and may be used for setting brick, stonework, and preparing a bed upon which tile is set. Unlike concrete, mortar does not have aggregate (smooth rocks of various sizes, up to about ¾ inch). Grout is a form of mortar.

Mudsill-The 2x4 or 2x6 section of lumber that is bolted to the foundation as the very first framing member. It must be pressure treated or foundation grade redwood.

Mullion-a strip that divides, or appears to divide, the panes of glass in a window. With many dual pane windows, a faux mullion is placed in the dead air space between the panes of glass.

Negative slope-a slope or grade that runs in the wrong direction, causing water to flow opposite of the direction that is intended (see **Slope**).

OSB-initials meaning oriented strand board. OSB is a manufactured wood product that comes in sheets measuring 4 feet wide by 8, 9, or 10 feet in length. OSB can be part of the house frame on the subfloor, walls or roofs. It is always covered by the finish flooring, siding, or roofing material.

PVC-a plastic pipe made from polyvinyl chloride. The most extensive use of this pipe is for irrigation supply lines. Other uses include storm and sewer piping. If the manufacturer adds another step to the process, called CPVC, the pipe can be used for cold-water household use in most locations.

Pad-a term used to describe the flat spot on a graded lot where the condominium or house is to be built. A padded lot refers to a lot that has been graded flat in one or more elevations and usually is certified by a civil engineer. It is also the material installed under the carpet.

Parapet-a low wall that extends above the edge of a roof and often found on the sides of decks and balconies.

Particle board-a a synthetic wood product which consists of a mixture of wood chips, sawdust and a glue-like binder called resin. It is manufactured in boards like lumber, or sheets like plywood, and has a broad range of applications in residential construction. Examples are shelving, door cores, and backing (underlayment) for tile and vinyl flooring. A related product, called oriented strand board (OSB), is used as roof underlayment and shear panels.

Patio-see Flatwork.

Pavers-pieces of stone, concrete, or brick that are placed side-by-side to form walkways and driveways. Shapes can be square, rectangular, hexagonal or other geometric shapes. Depending on the specific use, pavers are set over a base of sand, concrete, or mortar. **Penny-**a measurement of the size of nails. Derived from Old English system of measuring weight.

Perforated pipe-pipe that has holes or slots through the sidewall of the pipe to permit the collection of subterranean drainage water or the discharge of wastewater in a septic tank system leach field.

Pier-a column of concrete that extends down into the ground and is often attached to the underside of the grade beam. Sometimes an "independent" pier may be attached to the underside of the subfloor joists in the crawl space. The purpose of the pier is to provide additional load carrying capacity to the foundation.

Pitch-also known as slope, is the amount of drop (or rise) of a building component such as a roof, or deck. For example a roof that has a 5 and 12 pitch means that for every 12 feet of horizontal measurement the roof would rise up 5 feet in vertical measurement.

Plant on-an architectural feature that is usually glued or fastened to the exterior of a house to add dimension and character to walls and windows. Used frequently in stucco applications.

Plaster-see Stucco.

Plumb-a term given to a wall that is perfectly straight up and down. Out of plumb means that the wall is tilted to some measured extent.

Ponding-a condition where flat surfaces that are supposed to drain collect water in depressed areas called ponds (also called birdbaths).

Post-a vertical structural element larger than a stud used in the framing of a house. Posts are usually the vertical support for horizontal beams. Posts can also be found as a component in handrails.

Pot shelf-an architectural feature found on the inside and outside of some houses which is used for the placement of pots. They are often found in hallways and in bedrooms above closets, as well as on the exterior in front of windows.

Pre-emergent-a chemical that is applied to landscape areas in winter and to prevent weed seeds from sprouting.

Pressure treated-a chemical treatment given to lumber that may or will come in contact with the earth (ground). The process often gives a greenish or brownish color to the wood and linear perforations ("pickling marks") on the sides. Mudsills and fence posts are examples of lumber that should be pressure treated.

Primer-refers to the base coat or initial coat of a liquid, usually paint, sometimes resin, which penetrates and adheres to the coated object and provides a compatible surface for finish coats.

R-Value-the measurement of the ability of a substance to gain or lose heat. Insulation is rated by its R-Value. The higher the R-Value (like R-11, R-22, R-38 etc.), the greater ability to insulate.

Rafter-the common structural lumber used to create the frame of the roof. The rafters define the shape of the roof as well as the slope.

Rebar-the steel rods that are placed in a form, such as a foundation, to give added strength and resistance to prevent concrete cracking.

Refractory-a term given to ceramic or brick-like material made to withstand heat. Many fireplaces have precast panels of refractory material at the sides and back.

Riser-the vertical, back piece of a stair step that separates one tread from another.

Roof-the upper most structural component of the house or the building frame. A number of other terms are associated with roofs:

- **Gable-**a simple design of pitched roofs having a high point (called the ridge) and a low point (at the eave).
- **Hip-**a gable roof that has been clipped back at its outer end and with a sloped roof added to the clipped area.
- **Mansard-**a small, steeply pitched portion found around the perimeter of low pitched or flat roofs as an element of architectural enhancement.
- **Rake-**the line of the roof running from the ridge to the eave. Rakes can occur at the ends of gables, or where two sections of roof join in a hip.
- **Ridge-**the highest horizontal part of the roof.
- **Shed-**a pitched roof where the upper most part terminates at a wall or that begins at the top of a wall and is pitched in only one direction (as opposed to a gable roof which is pitched in two directions).
- **Valley-** is the opposite of **hip**. The valley is the low point where two roof planes intersect.

Roof cover-while the roof is part of the house or building structure, the roof cover is the material that gives the water shedding or water repellency nature to the roof. Examples of roof covers are noted:

- **Asphalt composition or shingle-**consists of a combination of fiberglass or felt with a petroleum product and finishes the outer surface with granulated sand, stone or other hard substances. Applied in strips about 3 feet long.
- **Built up roof-**also known as low pitch or flat roofs. The most common material used in this type of roof is hot asphalt (tar) mopped over a felt membrane and covered with gravel. Other materials used include rubber sheeting and elastomeric coatings.
- **Tile-**individual pieces made from mortar (concrete) or terra cotta. The material can be colored in the manufacturing process and it comes glazed or unglazed. Shapes include flat pieces (known as shakes), interlocking "S" shapes, or semicircular barrels.
- **Wooden shake or wooden shingle-**usually made from split cedar logs and hand applied on the roof one at a time.

Rosette-the two circular end pieces (usually plastic) mounted on the side wall of a closet. The purpose of a rosette is to provide the niche into which the closet pole is inserted. Also, a rosette is the round portion of the door hardware used to trim out the hole bored through the door.

Scalloping-an unacceptable condition of finished boards (including flooring) where the saw has made irregular cuts or chips out of the surface of the board.

Screw drive-the method of operation of some garage door opener mechanisms. Also known as worm drive. The screw drive is a long steel rod that runs between the opener and the door header and it revolves in a clockwise and counterclockwise direction.

Seismic-a term frequently used in conjunction with earthquake activity. Seismic design, which focuses on making the house stronger and less prone to damage in an earthquake, is a part of the Building Code. Some seismic building methods include tying the house to the foundation with long metal straps and using shear panels to keep the house from moving back and forth during an earthquake.

Sheathing-the part of the roof that covers the rafters. Sheathing is usually plywood or similar wood product. Strip sheathings are strips of 1 x 3 inch or 1 x 4 inch boards that are nailed across the rafters to provide a nailing surface for shingles and shakes.

Sheetrock®-see Drywall.

Shower pan-the bottom part of a shower. It may have been installed as a single unit or tiled over a waterproofing system.

Siding-the exterior covering of a house. Many materials can be used for siding, including wood, brick, vinyl, aluminum, plaster (stucco), and cement board.

Sill-the bottom of a window or patio door that is often confused with the trim piece, known as the stool, which is placed on the sill. Another sill, known as the mudsill, is the first piece of horizontal framing that is bolted to the foundation. Mudsills are required to be of termite resistant wood.

Slab-a term given to flat concrete and is often linked with a foundation type known as slab on grade. Slab is also used in reference to the floor of a garage or basement known as the garage slab and basement slab.

Slope-sometimes referred to as pitch or "fall". The percentage or angle of a surface (such as a patio, driveway, or the grading around the house) drops, as one moves outward from the house. When dealing with plumbing pipes the term "fall" is used, which means the percentage or degree of inclination of the pipe.

Soffit-an architectural term given to a roof projection that has had the underside enclosed so that the rafters cannot be seen. Overhead decks and walkways may be designed and constructed to provide soffits.

Sole plate-the 2x4 or 2x6 (sometimes 4x4 or 4x6) section of lumber that is laid flat on the slab or subfloor with the wall studs attached to the plate. In the case of a concrete slab, the sole plate and the mudsill are the same.

Spalling-the chipping or flaking of the exterior surface of a building material, usually concrete, that deeply pits the surface of the material. Concrete is known to spall in cold climates where the surface is subjected to repeated wetting and freezing. Cement plaster (stucco) can also spall for the same reason. Spalling can also occur in concrete when it is allowed to dry out (cure) too quickly.

Spark arrester-a metal screen-like device mounted on top of the chimney to prevent hot ashes from passing into the atmosphere and creating a fire hazard.

Splash block-a shallow trough with one open end placed under the discharge of a downspout to direct rainwater away from the foundation. Splash blocks are usually made of cast concrete, but they can also be made of cast fiberglass and metal.

Spores-are rapidly reproducing microscopic organisms that give rise to new adult molds, mildews and fungi. Found in mushrooms, ferns, mosses and other organic material.

Stool-the piece of trim that sits horizontally on the sill of a window. Often accompanied with a companion piece underneath it known as an apron. "Stool" can also refer to the lower piece of a toilet. Two piece toilets have a tank to hold the flushing water and a stool to receive the waste.

Stoop-a step (or series of steps) with a landing that leads to the exterior door of a house.

Storm collar-a piece of metal that looks like a clerical collar and is attached to the chimney cap or vent from a gas appliance. The flue runs through the storm collar.

Strike-the portion of door and cabinet hardware that is attached to the frame and receives the latch (through a hole in it) when the door is closed.

Stringer-the side boards on either side of a stairway. Unless the stairway is open, the treads run from one stringer across to the other.

Stucco-the hard weather resistant exterior surface of a house that has been applied by troweling or spraying. Stucco can be a form of mortar, known as cement plaster (sand and cement) or it can be a more synthetic material consisting of plastic resins and materials to bind them together. Many final textures are available for stucco including skip trowel, sand float, and brocade.

Stud-the common vertical structural pieces which support the walls of a house. Studs, usually wood but can be steel, are mostly 2 x 4 or 2 x 6-inches in cross dimension.

Subdrain-a drain that is placed underground to catch and divert subsurface water.

Subfloor-the flat flooring material connected to the floor joists. It is often made of plywood or several plywood substitutes. The finish floor, such as carpet, hardwood, tile, or linoleum, covers the subfloor.

Subpanel-a large electrical box with a metal or plastic door usually found mounted in the wall inside the house or garage. The subpanel contains the circuit breakers or fuses of the branch electrical circuits. Houses may have more than one subpanel. The main panel is the box on the outside of the house that contains the electric meter and possibly some circuit breakers.

Subsurface water- A distant source of water that passes underground through the soil causing the soil to slide and swell. Subsurface water has the potential to create stability problems for houses.

Swale-a surface path for seasonal water flow that can be natural or man-made. Often swales are cut around houses as part of the finished grading process to allow rainwater to flow away from the house and out toward the street.

Sweat-the process by which copper piping is joined together. Using a torch, the parts to be joined are heated and the solder flows into the joint. This process is known as "sweating" pipes.

Swing-sometimes known as hand, the term describes whether a door swings to the right or the left as you face it and open it toward you. Left-hand doors open and swing to the left and right hand doors open and swing to the right. Swing is an important thing to know when replacing doorknobs.

Tack strip-a narrow strip of wood with specialized nails driven through it in the opposite direction of the anchor nails, designed to catch and hold the edge of carpet. Tack strips are about 1 inch wide and up to 8 feet long and are nailed to the subfloor or concrete floor around the perimeter of a room. Protruding through the wood strips are sharp ends of specialized tacks. These tacks grab the carpet backing as the carpet is stretched toward the wall.

Tannins-an acidic and dark colored substance found in many plants and trees. Tannins will leach when the material is wetted or crushed. Two materials with significant tannins are redwood and oak wood.

Threshold-a piece of wood, metal, or plastic that is placed on the bottom of the exterior door opening to direct water away from the opening.

Toe kick-a small piece of wood at the bottom of cabinets, usually about 4 inches high, which lifts the cabinet off the floor and is recessed behind the cabinet face.

Trap-the piece of waste pipe just below sinks (visible), tubs and showers (not visible) which is shaped like a "U" or a "P". Traps retain some of the waste water and prevent sewer gases from backing into the house.

Tread-the flat part of a step.

Trench drain-a subterranean drainage trench that contains a perforated pipe at the bottom and is filled with a gravel mix. The term is often mistakenly interchanged with "French Drain" which is a gravel filled trench without the pipe.

Trim-a generic term given to material that "finishes off" or dresses up a house. Various examples of trim are baseboard, door casings, window stools and aprons, crown molding, wood applied to the exterior around windows, and material that is applied to the house (usually wood) after the stucco or siding has been installed.

Truss-a structural component engineered and manufactured to carry the weight of a floor or the weight of a roof. Trusses are often substituted for common floor joists and common rafters.

UL label-a label affixed to electrical appliances that have passed the independent tests administered by Underwriters Laboratory.

Underlayment-sheet of material, usually plywood, particle board, or cement board that is placed underneath the product that covers them to give rigidity. Used in roofing and flooring applications. The underlayment, if coated, can serve as a membrane.

Useful life-the term given to how long a particular component or product is supposed to last. Useful lives are provided by manufacturers, insurance companies, and industry groups based upon actual experience and testing.

Vapor barrier-a sheet membrane that has numerous applications to keep moisture from entering (or in some cases leaving) a house. Vapor barriers are installed on the exterior of the frame of a house prior to the application of siding or stucco. Building paper serves as a vapor barrier prior to the installation of lath and stucco. Concrete slabs are poured over a plastic vapor barrier to keep moisture in the ground moving up through the concrete via capillary action. In colder climates interior vapor barriers are put in the inside of exterior walls under the drywall to keep the humidity of the house at a constant level.

Vaulted ceiling-a ceiling that follows the pitch of the roof or the underside of the truss.

Veneer-a thin layer of finished material applied over a much thicker layer of core material. It is a common practice for door, cabinets, and furniture manufactures to place a veneer of fine wood over a core of particle board as part of their manufacturing process. Veneers can also be brick or masonry products.

Vents-there are many types of vents found in homes. Here are some of the more common ones:

- **Attic-**attic vents are usually louvered, often round, and found underneath the gables of a roof. Attic vents allow heat to escape during summer months.
- **Foundation-**foundation vents are installed with pier and grade beam foundations. These vents allow air to circulate and moisture to escape.
- **Plumbing-**plumbing vents are pipes that stick up through the roof and allow wastewater to pass through the house plumbing without becoming air locked.
- **Soffit-**vents that are found on the underside of soffits. They may be round, rectangular or narrow.
- **Window-**that portion of the window that opens and closes is called the vent.

Walkthrough-a practice used by builders when a house is delivered to the homeowner. A representative of the builder walks through the house with the homeowner prior to delivery. Often the builder will demonstrate the features of the house and give the homeowner instructions on care and maintenance. This event is also a very important opportunity for the homeowner to note any items that are incomplete or unacceptable. For example, countertop scratches and marks on the walls will probably not be covered under a builder's limited warranty once the homeowner takes possession of the house.

Wall-the exterior and interior vertical component system of a house. There are many types of walls and several examples are described here:

- ❑ **Bearing wall-**a wall that carries a portion of the weight of the house. Most exterior walls are bearing walls. Some interior walls are also bearing walls.
- ❑ **Headwall-**not a wall in a house, but a wall that has been constructed as part of a storm drain channel or piping system. The headwall is the concrete wall that serves as the beginning of a system where rain and storm water will flow from a channel into a system of piping.
- ❑ **Nonbearing wall-**a wall that is a partition between rooms, but does not carry the weight of any portion of the structure above it.
- ❑ **Party wall-**a wall where most likely two walls are constructed to separate one condominium from another or one townhouse from another. Also known as common walls, these walls must be constructed according to a specific standard in the Building Code.
- ❑ **Rated wall (Ceiling)-**a wall that has been constructed to meet certain fire resistive and noise transmission standards.
- ❑ **Shear wall-**a wall of a house that has been reinforced against back and forth movement (caused by earthquakes and wind forces) using sheets of plywood, oriented strand board, or other materials approved by the Building Code.

Water hammer-the action of water under high pressure, rushing through pipes and hitting a turn in the piping or a closed valve. Water hammer makes a banging noise in the piping. It can eventually break the piping connections and cause the piping to come loose. A common water hammer problem is the electric valves on a washing machine closing quickly between cycles.

Waterproofing-a term given to plastic and rubbery building materials that keep water from penetrating surfaces such as windows, retaining walls, and certain stucco surfaces.

Weatherstripping-material made of plastic, felt, rubber, and metal that are placed around the frames of doors and windows to provide a final seal against the intrusion of wind and rain.

Weep holes-a small hole found at the exterior side of most windows to allow rainwater to exit from the channel of the window onto the outside of the building.

Weep screed-a strip of metal, used as part of stucco applications, running parallel to the ground, about 6 inches off the ground where the stucco terminates. Rainwater that may be trapped behind the stucco will run down the building paper and exit through the weep screed.

References

California Department of Toxic Substances Control, M.B. Gilbert Associates, et. al., *Homeowners Guide to Earthquake Safety and Environmental Hazards*, California Department of Real Estate and California EPA, 2002.

Demske, Richard, *Plumbing*, Grosset & Dunlap, New York, NY, 1975.

Gerhart, James, *Caring for Your Home, A Guide to Maintaining Your Investment*, BuilderBooks, Washington, D.C., 1998.

Hrin, Tom et.al., *Your New Home and How To Take Care of It*, Home Builder Press, Washington, D.C., 2001.

MacLellan, David E. et. al., *California Building Performance Guidelines for Residential Construction*, The Building Standards Institute, Sacramento, CA, 2002.

MacLellan, David E. et. al., *The Home Book*, The Building Standards Institute, Sacramento, CA 2014.

Maguire, Jack, *500 Terrific Ideas for Home Maintenance and Repair*, Galahad Books, NY, 1991.

Sacks, Alvin M., *Residential Water Problems*, NAHB Home Builder Press, Washington, DC, 1994.

Tenenbaum, David J., *The Complete Idiot's Guide to Trouble Free Home Repair*, Alpha Books, NY, 1996.